DIVERSITY

AND COMPLEXITY

PRIMERS IN COMPLEX SYSTEMS

DIVERSITY
AND COMPLEXITY

Scott E. Page

PRINCETON UNIVERSITY PRESS
Princeton & Oxford

Published by Princeton University Press,
41 William Street, Princeton, New Jersey 08540
In the United Kingdom: Princeton University Press,
6 Oxford Street, Woodstock, Oxfordshire OX20 1TW

Jacket art by Uros Krcadinac (www.krcadinac.com/synesketch)

ISBN (pbk.) 978-0-691-13767-4
Library of Congress Control Number: 2010936220

British Library Cataloging-in-Publication Data is available

This book has been composed in Adobe Garamond and Helvetica neue
Printed on acid-free paper. ∞
press.princeton.edu

Typeset by S R Nova Pvt Ltd, Bangalore, India
Printed in the United States of America

5 7 9 10 8 6 4

CONTENTS

ACKNOWLEDGMENTS

I have many people and places to thank for their assistance with my efforts on this book. A decision by the Santa Fe Institute and Princeton University Press to create a series of books demonstrating the advances in the science of complexity was the impetus for this particular book. Elementary physics informs us that a slight push can have a large effect provided that the object sits atop a big hill. For me, that hill (literally) was a year spent at the Center for Advanced Studies in the Behavioral Sciences at Stanford. The center afforded me the time and space needed to complete a rough draft. My return to the University of Michigan provided a yearlong "author meets critics" session that improved the text that follows. A USAF MURI grant and NSF IGERT and HSD grants provided funding to allow me to workshop portions of the text as well.

In researching this book, I gained renewed respect for the scholarship of many people, most notably, Simon Levin, Steven Frank, Rick Riolo, David Krakauer, Jenna Bednar, Bobbi Low, Melanie Mitchell, and Martin Weitzman. A book of this scope demands broad strokes and limited detail. Many times, I felt as though I stood before a paint by numbers canvas holding a spray gun. One cannot help but feel one's own sweeping attempt to contribute to be inadequate by comparison with the detailed care with which these scholars approach questions.

I wish to especially thank John Miller, whose vision inspired this series, and Chuck Myers, for cracking the whip and editing the text. Without Chuck, this project might not have been finished until May 2014. Throughout the writing, Howard Oishi and Mita Gibson prevented me from spiraling into an administrative abyss. Without the suggestions, critiques, and ideas of many friends and colleagues who've contributed to this project, I doubt I'd have finished it. Simon Levin, Rajiv Sethi, Bill Clark, Sarah Cherng, Jenna Bednar, and P. J. Lamberson commented on earlier drafts of this book and found some glaring errors in fact and logic. Andrea Jones-Rooy worked through the entire text and relieved the reader of twenty-seven and a half tedious paragraphs and two hundred and sixteen unnecessary flowery adjectives. Evan Economo gave a near final draft a thorough reading and identified no fewer than eleven places where I would have offended natural scientists. Thanks to all.

I've dedicated this book to a diverse, complex pair of muses: Stan Reiter and Carl Simon. Over the years, Stan and Carl, along with their partners Nina and Bobbi, have offered guidance, wisdom, patience, and love to me and to my family.

To Orrie and Cooper, my constant reminders of the complexity that diversity can produce, I marvel at your abilities to find and produce joy. And to Jenna, as our continuous lives increase in dimensionality and depth, you remain the helium in my balloons, the peach in my cobbler, and the warm home at the end of the prairie's winding path.

DIVERSITY

AND COMPLEXITY

PRELUDE: THE MEANING OF DIVERSITY

The diversity of the phenomena of nature is so great, and
the treasures hidden in the heavens so rich, precisely in
order that the human mind shall never be lacking
in fresh nourishment.
—JOHANNES KEPLER

In writing this book, I have been fortunate to be guided and motivated by the efforts of an incredible collection of scholars. The study of diversity and complexity attracts a vast array of scholars from multiple disciplines whose passion, intelligence, and energy inspire awe. In what follows, I attempt to pull together ideas, concepts, models, and results that intersect with the topics of diversity and complexity, and to make sense of research from multiple disciplines. It proves a daunting, humbling, and ultimately, exciting task.

The book combines illustrative examples, formal models, and bits of data to produce an overview of the interplay between diversity and complexity. The relationship between the two is not always easy to understand. Diversity and complexity lie at the core of many of the challenges that we currently face: managing ecosystems, organizations, and economies. Progress in these domains or, more modestly, continued survival can only benefit from a more nuanced understanding of diversity in complex systems, and that requires naming the parts and learning how those parts combine. It means that we must go beyond stories and analogies. We have to test intuitions and metaphors against logic and empirical reality. For example, it's not enough to say "diversity enhances robustness." If we are to take intelligent action, we need to define our terms precisely—what is diversity? and what is robustness?

For those people who feel diversity to be of paramount importance for the continued flourishing of societies, economies, and ecosystems, I hope that this book provides theoretical foundations to support that passion. A warning though: the book challenges the naïve assumption that we should always prefer more diversity to less. Too much diversity, as I show in several places, can produce catastrophe or inefficiency. Rotating the presidency of the European Council between a few countries has advantages. Leadership diversity produces innovative policies and prevents the concentration of power. Rotating it among dozens of countries, though, may create policy instability (Kollman 2003). Even if on balance diversity's a good thing, we can have too much of it.

For those people who do deep scientific work within a particular discipline, accept my apologies that this book covers a lot of territory that you already know. But it will also, I hope, introduce a few new measures, concepts, models, and theories from other disciplines that spark new ideas. Working across the disciplines requires translating formal language (one person's epistatic interaction is another person's externality or spillover), suffering through notational conventions, and learning implicit assumptions. My not so secret hope is that this book introduces some ideas that "jump the silo" of their home discipline and advance interdisciplinary science.

The title of this prelude, "the meaning of diversity", should evoke three interpretations: *importance*, *essence*, and *averaging*. The importance of diversity in complex systems is the central theme of this book. Why does diversity matter? What roles does it play? I show that diversity has many roles and effects. Diversity can provide insurance, improve productivity, spur innovation, enhance robustness, produce collective knowledge, and, perhaps most important in light of these other effects, sustain further diversity. But diversity, for all its benefits, is no panacea: It can contribute to collapse, conflict, and incomprehensible mangles.

As for essence, in the next chapter I struggle with how to categorize types of diversity. Eventually, I distinguish between three types: *variation within* a type, differences *across* types, and differences *between* communities or systems. Each of these types can be measured in several ways and each has distinct functions within complex systems. Variation allows for local search, provides responsiveness to minor changes in the environment, and serves as an engine for diversity of types. Diversity across types creates synergies. It allows the whole to be more than the parts. And diversity between communities provides robustness to major changes.

As for averaging, I mean to provoke. Empirical scientists— be they social, physical, or natural—often rely on statistical techniques to make sense of the world. Statistical regressions, for the most part, report means (averages). Means reveal general tendencies that can be misleading. For that reason, economists, especially those interested in policy effects, have increasingly turned to quantile regression techniques (Koenker and Hallock 2001). Quantile regression enables empirical scientists to estimate effects in different parts of the distribution. For example, the average effect of an increase in the gasoline tax can be determined for different segments of the income distribution. Rather than estimate a society-wide mean effect, quantile regression can estimate the effect on the median person in the bottom fifth of the distribution, the next fifth, and so on.

In a complex system with feedbacks, the system generally cannot be approximated by an aggregate variable (Osgood 2008; Iwasa, Andreasen, and Levin 1987). If 1 percent of the population earns 50 percent of the income, an increase in average income need not be indicative of broadly improving welfare. It might just mean that the rich have become richer. A book, such as this, that focuses on diversity pushes back against the tendency toward averaging both for pragmatic reasons—to highlight the value of looking beyond means— and for aesthetics—to call attention to what Janet Malcolm (2008) calls "the gorgeousness of the particulars of the things that are alive in the world."

This book is about diversity and complexity. I'll start with diversity. The single word that jumps to mind in thinking about diversity is *wonder*. When I read research by ecologists who document the diversity of ants and orchids or studies by anthropologists that richly describe differences in human cultures, experiences, and languages, I have a common reaction. I'm awed by the beauty and the intricacies of those differences, and by the curious balance of randomness and assembly. Take humans. We combine idiosyncratic frozen accidents (why not six toes?) and highly functional parts like the lung and the brain. Some differences seem necessary; other differences seem, well, like oddities.

My analysis of diversity starts with two questions: what is it, and why do we see it? To tackle the first question, I survey various measures of diversity. Ecologists, physicists, and statisticians measure diversity differently. By putting all the measures in a common framework, I make it easier to see the strengths and biases of each. I found attempting to answer the second question—why we see diversity and why we don't—to be a lot of fun. We accept without much thought that at restaurants soda pop comes in three sizes, beer comes in two, and wine comes in one. But why?

One day on the University of Michigan's Central Campus, I decided to look at the diversity in the color of male students' pants. I found that over 90 percent wore either blue, black, or khaki pants. By any measure of diversity (and I present a bunch in the text) that's not much. If I were to do the same experiment in Amsterdam, I'd get much more diversity. Why? Or, consider that entomologists have identified nearly 15,000 species of ants and estimate double that number exist, but chemistry identifies fewer than two hundred elements. Again, why?

I end up dividing the "why do we see diversity" question into two parts. I first consider the causes of diversity. How does it get produced? I cover a complete set of causes in the text, but will mention two here. In human systems, one obvious cause is slippage (Bednar 2006). Mistakes happen. Those mistakes create variation and variations accumulate into difference. Another cause is creation. People just think up the coolest stuff: the Fosbury Flop, the sonnet, and that miniature three-legged plastic table that keeps the pizza box top from collapsing.

I then consider constraints. Given the many sources of diversity, without constraints we'd have too much of it. These constraints transcend disciplines. For any type of entity, there exists a size of the possible. One can imagine many types of houses but not many types of ball bearings. Physics also constrains diversity. The bones needed to support a five-hundred-foot tall human would weigh so much, the person couldn't move. So, we can't (as much as I used to like to think it) be living in a *Horton Hears a Who* world, in which we reside on a speck on a dandelion in a much larger world. I cover other constraints in the book. Here, I just want to make clear that it's possible to construct logic that partly explains why we see the diversity that we do.

After writing what amounts to a brief, interdisciplinary primer on diversity, I then turn to understanding the functions of diversity in complex systems. At this point, I should provide some background on complexity and complex systems (Miller and Page 2008; Epstein 2006; Mitchell 2009). By complexity, I mean elaborate temporal and spatial patterns and structures. Complex phenomena are hard to describe, explain, or predict—like the weather or the economy. I provide formal definitions of complexity in greater detail later, but these will do for now.

To get a feel for complex phenomena, we also need to understand the systems that produce them. Complex systems are collections of diverse, connected, interdependent entities whose behavior is determined by rules, which may adapt, but need not. The interactions of these entities often produce phenomena that are more than the parts. These phenomena are called *emergent*. Given this characterization, the brain would count as a complex system, so would a rainforest, and so would the city of Baltimore. Each contains diverse, connected entities that interact. Each produces outcomes that exceed the capacities of its component parts. Neurons are simple. Brains are complex.

By way of comparison, a calculus exam and a blender would not be complex, though for different reasons. The parts of a calculus exam—the questions—don't interact. It's a fixed set of problems, so it may be *difficult* but it won't be complex (Page 2008). The blender won't be complex either, but for a different reason. It cannot adapt. Yes, it has diverse parts, and those parts follow rules governed by physical and mechanical laws, but those rules don't allow it to respond to the environment. As a result, the blender itself is a fixed-number-of-tricks pony: blend, puree, and liquefy. It cannot toast bread or make french fries. A blender, like most machines, is therefore *complicated*. The line dividing complex and complicated gets blurry in places. I would classify Boeing's 787 airplane, which uses flight guidance software, as complex. Others might see it as complicated.

Unlike blenders, most complex systems are not predictable. Owing to the interdependence of actions, complex systems can be predicted only in the very short run. Maps from genotype to phenotype, weather patterns, and economies are all complex and not easily forecast even with abundant data (Orrell 2007). The particulars that emerge within complex systems are also difficult to predict. Who could have expected the koala, the macarena, or Super Mario Brothers? As for stability, though often robust, complex systems are also capable of producing large events, such as mass extinctions (Erwin 2006; Newman 1997) and stock market crashes. Owing to the interactions between entities, complex systems produce these large events far more often than would be predicted by "normal" that is, Gaussian fluctuations.

As a result, complexity creates problems for analysis. In systems that produce static equilibria, we can gauge the effect of changing levels of diversity by performing *comparative static analysis*. We can measure how the equilibrium changes when diversity is increased or decreased, and we can quantify the effect. We can say things like "increasing the diversity of preferences results in price increases." In systems that produce complex outcomes, such as long transients with emergent patterns, we cannot make such simple comparisons. For that reason, examples in which diversity has isolatable, direct effects prove rare. And any foray into scholarly research on the impact of diversity in complex systems proves a humbling experience.

That said, some broad general claims do appear to hold across contexts. First, diversity often enhances the robustness of complex systems. By robustness, I mean the ability to maintain functionality (Jen 2005) rather than analytic stability. Systems that lack diversity can lose functionality. History has many examples of failure through lack of diversity, the potato famine being among the more notable.[1] The potato must be counted among the most precious of the gifts introduced into Europe during the age of exploration. Of the thousands of varieties of potato grown in Central and South America at their disposal, the Europeans imported primarily two. This lack of genetic variation presented a huge target for parasites. When the potato blight hit, it found field upon field of genetically similar potatoes. Though nearly a million Irish perished, even more relocated to America. Diversity at the community level—America had a different mix of crops from Ireland—minimized the global impact of the blight. Had every country been subsisting on potatoes as Ireland had, the famine would have been an even worse calamity.

Second, diversity drives innovation and productivity. In biology, the forces of mutation and recombination are well known to be primary sources of innovation. In economies, variation and experimentation also lead to innovation, and, as Arthur (2009) convincingly shows, so does recombination. In fact, recombination may be the biggest driver of economic and scientific innovation. As for productivity, I've covered some of this terrain in an earlier book (Page 2007a), but it's worth repeating. Whether one looks at ecosystems, empires, or cities, greater diversity for the most part correlates with greater productivity. Cities that are more diverse are more productive and more innovative.

The productivity and efficiency of ecosystems are harder to measure. Among other approaches, the efficiency of ecosystems can be measured by how effectively they degrade energy. A barren rocky flat degrades energy from the sun less effectively than a forest (Schneider and Kay 1994). I'm taking an aggregate view here. In the case of ecosystem productivity, the relationship varies depending on the scale of the ecosystems and other factors. The same holds for cities: size matters. Thus, any broad claim of correlation such as these will have many counterexamples.

To show how diversity produces benefits, we need not identify synergies and superadditivities. As I show in the book, diversity improves productivity for two rather mundane reasons: averaging and diminishing returns to type. Averaging enables diverse systems to perform well regardless of the state of the world.

Diminishing returns are a widespread phenomenon. Whether one looks at ecosystems and frequency-dependent fitness or firms and diminishing returns to scale, one finds that at some point having more of the same produces diminishing productivity. And, given that diminishing returns implies a benefit to diversity, we should not be at all surprised that productivity correlates with diversity. In fact, I might even go so far as to say that when we don't see diversity producing benefits—such as in some diverse groups of people—we should go looking for a cause. To wit, diverse groups sometimes perform poorly. Often, their failure can be attributed to an inability to communicate or a lack of trust.

Finally, to step away for a moment from objective scientific criteria, diversity merits attention because, at least subjectively, it makes systems more interesting. Diversity is why London or New York is more exciting than Duluth. Why the earth is more interesting than the moon. Why the Amazon rainforest is more interesting than a field of soybeans and an opera is more interesting than a ballad. Diversity alone, though, is not enough. Interestingness requires the right connections and interactions. And those have to be assembled through evolution or through judicious practice (Alexander 2001). Otherwise, we just get gray goo—an incomprehensible mess.

The salience of diversity and complexity in the modern, connected world provides a reason to read this book. Many of the challenges that we presently face—climate change, epidemics, terrorism, segregation, global economic disparities, financial markets, and international policy—involve complex systems. Each challenge involves anticipating and harnessing diverse, adaptive entities, with interdependent actions. These entities interact within contact structures or networks. Actions taken at one time and place often echo across networks of relationships. Small events can trigger large reactions—a football fan forgets a camera, runs back through airport security, and delays hundreds of flights across the United States. And, as mentioned above, within diverse complex systems, large events can often be absorbed with minimal loss of function. For example, the 2009 earthquake near L'Aquila, Italy, wiped out buildings and roads, leaving 70,000 people homeless. Italy's economy, though already in bad shape, took a hit but did not collapse.

The complexity of our challenges arises from the increasing connectedness of the human world. When interactions were few and far between—when farmers went to market a couple of times a year, when armies and crusaders moved by foot and wagon, and when ideas spread primarily by word of mouth, the resulting systems were more episodic than complex. The transition from episodic histories—from brief encounters to multilayered interactions—has been gradual and inexorable (Diamond 1999). I don't mean to imply that ideas and technologies did not spread. They surely did, but the spread was much slower. Technology has reduced distances between people. We cannot help but bump into other people who look, behave, and think differently. Today, as Thomas Friedman so aptly puts it, the world is flat—everything interacts with everything else, at least potentially.[2] The resulting complexity, whether it works for us or against us, depends to a large extent on the amount of diversity.

If we can understand how to leverage diversity to achieve better performance and greater robustness, we might anticipate and prevent collapses. To combine ideas from some of my University of Michigan colleagues (Axelrod and Cohen 2000; Holland 1998), if we hope to harness complexity, we need to identify lever points—points in time at which intervention can have large effects. To do that, we must undertake the relatively pedestrian exercises of defining the pieces and figuring out how those pieces fit together. Does this mean that we can prevent collapses such as the 2008 home mortgage crisis in the United States? Perhaps. That crisis partly resulted from a failure to recognize interdependence in the value of financial assets. An emphasis on complexity thinking might have made us more aware of the system's fragility.

By definition, complexity isn't easy to grasp. To grasp the role of diversity within a complex system can be even more challenging. For those reasons, much of what follows involves the use of simple models. Models take us farther than analogies and metaphors. Permit me two examples. The first involves rivets. Advocates of species preservation often invoke the analogy of rivets on an airplane. No one rivet is crucial, but if the plane loses too many rivets it won't hold together. This analogy makes an important point—losing lots of little things can have a big effect—but it's a crude model of an ecosystem. Rivets are all identical. Species differ. Rivets exhibit limited functional plasticity—they shrink and expand with temperature changes. Species can and do adapt to their environments in rich and often unpredictable ways. Understanding how a fixed system responds to the loss of a part doesn't tell us enough about how a complex system responds to the knockout of a species, an idea, or a firm.

The rivet analogy, therefore, is a start, but we have to dig more deeply. Models can help us understand whether the rivet analogy holds together or whether it cries wolf.

The second example involves disturbances. It seems intuitive that disturbances should help maintain diversity, as what works best at one moment in time may not be what performed best previously. Variation in the environment should keep multiple types alive—be those types species or firms. This intuition turns out to be incomplete, as I show when analyzing the *interim disturbance hypothesis*. However, if we just add a few more details—frequency-dependent fitness, spatial differentiation, etc., then the argument holds water. The analysis demonstrates the power of formal models. The math allows us to nail down our logic. Math is our friend.

Math, though, isn't the easiest of companions. It's austere and strict. Mathematical models come with costs. They can be difficult to follow. That may be especially true in a book such as this that borrows models from multiple disciplines. I ask the less technical readers to hang in there. This book is neither a quick read nor impenetrable, neither an airplane book nor a doorstop. It occupies a middle ground. If you must, skim the math on the first pass (I've put most of it in boxes), then go back and work through the particulars in more detail. The payoff will be a deeper, more precise understanding.

A book such as this cannot avoid the fact that the topic of diversity carries on its back some significant ideological baggage. Acts to save endangered species, proposals to increase or cease affirmative action, and appeals for cultural preservation all appeal to the benefits of diversity. These appeals often take the form of imperatives. I come with no hidden or explicit agenda. I come not to praise diversity but to explore. Understanding the relevance of diversity—especially to robustness—often requires thinking about complexity. By studying diversity and complexity together, we can start to say things about *what kind* of diversity, *when*, and *under what conditions* produces good outcomes (robustness) in systems with *what kinds* of characteristics.

That's not to say that a broad strokes approach such as this doesn't have limitations. Ideas and insights won't always transfer across contexts. An economy is not an ecosystem, and the human brain is not the Internet. The Internet doesn't have a frontal lobe and the human brain doesn't have email (at least not yet).

A critic could argue that because complex systems differ in their particulars, we cannot expect that the functions of diversity in one complex system translate to others. My first response to that position is that we should not aim for a theory that gets the details correct in every specific case, but instead pursue the more modest goal of identifying core functions of diversity—as responsiveness, as fuel, as insurance, etc. Those core insights will fan out across disciplines; they will apply within economies, ecosystems, and biological systems alike. To the extent my belief holds true, the pages that follow have greater value. My second response is that even if the attempt fails, the effort may be worthwhile. By pursuing common principles, we learn which particulars matter.

Furthermore, and this may be equally important, by studying diverse disciplines, we may find concepts and tools that we can apply fruitfully to our own. I cannot resist mentioning research by one of my colleagues at Michigan, Mercedes Pascual. She and Stefano Allesina decided to take Google's PageRank algorithm and apply it to ecosystems

(Allesina and Pascual 2009). They found that a species' PageRank was an excellent predictor of the likelihood that the extinction of that species would lead to secondary extinctions within an ecosystem. Their research can be seen as an example of *horizontal transfer*, which occurs when an idea or solution jumps from one domain to another. Horizontal transfer will be one of many ways in which diversity arises in complex systems. It can also be one of the ways that science advances.

I had two audiences in mind when writing this book. As mentioned, one is that large group of people who care deeply about diversity but who pick up technical journal articles and find themselves overwhelmed by jargon and notation. The second group consists of academics. That group can be divided into subgroups. One consists of individuals who work on issues related to diversity within a single discipline. Diversity spurs the interests of a variety of scholars: sociologists, political scientists, biologists, ecologists, and economists, to name just a few. Learning how other disciplines approach similar and related problems has been eye opening, and at times eye popping. I expect it will be for others as well. The second consists of scholars interested in complex systems who haven't unpacked the contributions of diversity to complexity. A third consists of undergraduate and graduate students looking for interesting research ideas. This book asks more question than it answers. I worry on its completion whether I've accomplished more than depositing puzzle pieces on the floor. If that turns out to be true, I hold out hope that young scholars with passion and vision will read this book and put some of those pieces together.

1

ON DIVERSITY AND COMPLEXITY

> Armageddon is not around the corner. This is only what
> the people of violence want us to believe. The complexity
> and diversity of the world is the hope for the future.
> —MONTY PYTHON'S MICHAEL PALIN

In this chapter, I pose and answer some basic questions. What is diversity? What is complexity? And, why link diversity and complexity—what does one have to do with the other? First, diversity. Diversity applies to populations or collections of entities. A ball bearing cannot be diverse. Nor can a flower. Diversity requires multitudes. Cities are diverse; they contain many people, organizations, buildings, roads, etcetera. Ecosystems are diverse because they contain multiple types of flora and fauna.

When scientists speak of diversity, they can mean any of three characteristics of a population. They can mean *variation* in some attribute, such as differences in the length of finches' beaks. They can mean *diversity* of types, such as different types of stores in a mall. Or they can mean differences in *configuration*, such as different connections between atoms in a molecule.

Complexity proves to be a much more problematic concept. As mentioned in the Prelude, complexity can be loosely thought of as interesting structures and patterns that are not easily described or predicted. Systems that produce complexity consist of *diverse* rule-following entities whose behaviors are *interdependent*. Those entities interact over a *contact structure* or *network*. In addition, the entities often *adapt*. That adaptation can be learning in a social system, or natural selection in an ecological system. I find it helpful to think of complex systems as "large" in Walt Whitman's sense of containing contradictions. They tend to be robust and at the same time capable of producing large events. They can attain equilibria, both fixed points and simple patterns, as well as produce long random sequences.

To provide an example of the type of analysis that follows, I begin with an example of how diversity contributes to complexity in economics. Imagine an exchange market— a bazaar in which people bring wheelbarrows of goods to trade. This example demonstrates how diversity can reduce volatility in a system and also produce complexity. In an exchange market, diversity can enter in three ways: (1) in what the agents bring to buy and sell, their *endowments*; (2) in the agents' *preferences* for the different goods; and (3) in the ways the agents *adapt* to information, specifically prices.

If the market had no diversity, not much would happen. If everyone had identical endowments and preferences, then no one would have any reason to trade. So, we need diversity on at least one of these dimensions just to make the market come to life. Let's add diversity to both endowments and preferences so that agents bring different goods to market and desire different bundles of goods as well. In such a market, we need some mechanism for prices to form. Following standard economics, let's assume that there exists a market maker, who calls out prices with the intent of producing equilibrium trades.

Once we introduce the market maker, we have to take into account how agents respond to prices. Let's start by assuming no diversity. If all of the agents react in the same way, then prices will be volatile. They'll jump all over the place. This volatility results from everyone reacting in the same way to a price that's too low, resulting in a massive increase in demand and a similar rise in price. Gintis (2007) shows that diversity in the learning rules reduces this volatility. Later in the book, I provide a simple model involving negative and positive feedbacks that explains the stabilizing effect of variability in responses. Here, I just wish to raise the point that diversity can stabilize.

This model can be made even more complex. Kirman and Vriend (2001) add realism by dispensing with the market maker. Instead, they allow individual buyers and sellers to strike up relationships with one another. With this added realism, diversity has more subtle effects. If buyers differ in the price at which they value the goods, then buyers with relatively high values tend to pay higher prices. Furthermore, high value buyers exhibit less loyalty than buyers with low values. In this model, diversity produces complexity through the web of connections and reputations that emerge from the system. Without diversity, nothing interesting happens. With diversity, we get relatively stable market prices, but when we look at the agents and how they behave, we see a complex system.

In the remainder of this chapter, I begin with brief overviews of what is meant by diversity and complexity. I then describe how diversity contributes to complexity with some specific examples including the spatial prisoner's dilemma. I conclude the chapter by describing what I call the *assemblage* problem—the fact that many complex systems are assembled, typically from the bottom up. The fact that complex systems are assembled complicates empirical tests of the benefits of diversity.

Characterizing Diversity

There are many ways to characterize diversity. Each affects how much diversity we see in a particular situation. I may walk into a furniture store and see tremendous diversity in style. You may walk in and see no diversity at all—just a bunch of bedroom furniture. In this section, I describe several categorizations of types of diversity as well as some common measures of diversity.

One logical starting place for thinking about how to categorize diversity is to distinguish between continuous and discrete differences. The weights of the members of a murder of crows or of a parliament of owls vary. These differences in weight can take on any real value; hence we can think of them as a continuous variable. Alternatively, we can think of diversity as the number of types or as the distribution across those types. For example, to capture diversity, we might count the number and types of animals in a zoo or species in a rainforest. The two approaches, measuring variation in weight and counting the number of types, capture different types of diversity. Many of the populations that interest us will include mixtures of discrete and continuous differences. Bluebirds differ from cardinals, but among the cardinals there exist continuous differences. Some cardinals appear just a little redder than others.

Though logically clean, the continuous/discrete dichotomy approach doesn't accord with how people typically categorize diversity. Instead, people more often distinguish between differences within a type (*variation*) and differences across types (*diversity*). The notion of types will prove problematic, but people like to create types or categories. Doing so allows us to make sense of the barrage of stimuli coming at us. (It's a bird, it's a plane, it's Superman!) I should note that the within/across types categorization mostly agrees with the continuous/discrete categorization. The two disagree primarily in cases where the differences within a type are discrete, such as differences in colors of paint.

In what follows, I will sometimes also refer to diversity of *compositions* or arrangement. A washing machine and an airplane engine may contain many of the same parts, but they differ in assembly. Putting all of this together gives three types of diversity.[3]

- *Diversity within a type, or* **variation**. *This refers to differences in the amount of some attribute or characteristic, such as the height of giraffes.*
- **Diversity** *of types and kinds, or species in biological systems. This refers to differences in kind, such as the different types of foods kept in a refrigerator.*
- *Diversity of* **composition**. *This refers to differences in how the types are arranged. Examples include recipes and molecules.*

Figure 1.1. Variation: Diversity within a type.

This trichotomy will prove helpful throughout the book as I analyze the effects of diversity. Like most classifications, this one seems great if you don't think about it too deeply. Once you do, problems begin to arise. Take the length of finches' beaks. These differences would seem to fall into the category of variation. However, an ecologist will counter with the fact that finches with different sized beaks eat different types of seeds and nuts and therefore occupy different places in the food network. So, perhaps, we might also think of them as different types. In sum, this categorization won't be perfect, but it provides enough structure for us to move forward.

Variation

Diversity within a type, or variation, is often defined along dimensions, such as length, width, height, circumference, or color. Suppose that you go on a scavenger hunt and find eight marbles. If you measure the diameters of those marbles, you would probably find that they are not all the same. They exhibit *variation* in their diameters.

Variation within a type plays important roles in the adaptability and robustness of complex systems. As I just mentioned, members of the same species exhibit variation in wing size and beak length, and those differences allow them to

Figure 1.2. Diversity across types.

occupy distinct niches. Not only can the differences produce a fitness or survivability advantage for some members of that species, they also allow the species to adapt to a changing environment.

Differences of Types

When people speak of diversity, they tend to mean differences of types. Suppose that instead of asking you to gather marbles, I asked you to search your house for circular objects. You might find a frisbee, a pizza pan, a dinner plate, and a quarter. This collection would contain *diverse types* of objects even though they are all circular.

These diverse circular objects have different functions. You could eat dinner off a frisbee, and you could play catch with a dinner plate, but neither would be much fun. The functional differences between quarters and pizza pans are even more extreme. You could cook a pizza on a quarter, but it wouldn't be very filling. And, no matter how hard you tried, you couldn't load a parking meter with a pizza pan. These differences in functionalities make the world more complex, as I shall show.

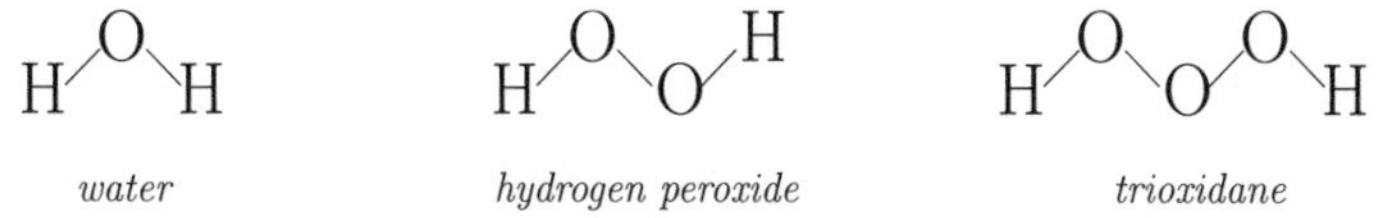

water   hydrogen peroxide   trioxidane

Figure 1.3. Diverse community compositions.

Differences in Community Composition

Finally, diversity can refer to differences in community or population composition. Water (H_2O) hydrogen peroxide (H_2O_2) and trioxidane (H_2O_3) all consist of combinations of hydrogen atoms and oxygen atoms, but differ in their relative amounts.

These differences in composition result in distinct emergent properties. Water has all sorts of interesting emergent properties, such as the tendency to form spheres when placed on a leaf or a freshly waxed surface, and even the ability to climb trees. Hydrogen peroxide, which differs from water by only one oxygen atom, is widely used as a disinfectant and as a whitener. It is also unstable. If exposed to sunlight it will decompose into water and oxygen, which is why it comes in brown bottles. Trioxidane, an oxidant that differs from hydrogen peroxide by only one oxygen atom, is also unstable. In the air it will decompose in a matter of minutes. If placed in water, it will decompose into a simple water molecule and an individual oxygen atom almost instantaneously.

Diversity of composition underpins much of the vast type diversity we observe in biology. The cells of all vertebrates come from only a few hundred or so types of cells. Humans, rats, and camels are comprised of muscle cells, nerve cells, glandular cells, and so on. Humans differ from rats not so much in the types of cells that we have, but in the proportions of those cells and in how those cells are arranged. That vertebrates are built from only a few cell types only moderately restricts the set of possible vertebrates. The vertebrates that presently exist are a tiny sample of what is possible (Jacob 1977).

The concept of diversity of composition provides an entrée into the concept of modularity. Many evolved and created systems are modular. Near the end of the penultimate chapter, I discuss how modularity promotes robustness. It's worth noting as well that modularity also simplifies the creation of diversity. Cars have modularized packages of extras. If you can choose from three engine modules, four stereo and communication modules, three interior models, and four trim modules, then you have a choice of one hundred and forty-four cars. The modularization is intended to guarantee that every one of those cars functions.

Complexity

Complexity has many definitions and measures. In the 1980s, Seth Lloyd began counting up definitions of complexity and stopped at forty or so (Lloyd 1988). The multitude of characterizations that Lloyd discovered reflects less a lack of agreement than an inability of any single approach to capture what scientists mean by complex. A similar problem exists for definitions of culture. Hundreds of definitions exist, and each has strengths and weaknesses. For both complexity and culture, a collection of definitions may well be needed to convey the essence of the term.

In discussing complexity, I will also devote time to describing complex systems. A complex system consists of *diverse* entities that interact in a *network* or *contact structure*—a geographic space, a computer network, or a market. These entities' actions are *interdependent*—what one protein, ant, person, or nation does materially affects others. In navigating within a complex system, entities follow rules, by which I mean prescriptions for certain behaviors in particular circumstances. These rules might be fixed: water molecules follow physical and chemical laws that are constant with respect to context.

Often, scholars distinguish between *complex systems*—systems in which the entities follow fixed rules—and *complex adaptive systems*—systems in which the entities adapt. If the entities adapt, then the system has a greater capacity to respond to changes in the environment. Adaptation occurs at the level of individuals or of types. The system itself doesn't adapt. The parts do; they alter their behaviors leading to system level adaptation.

Note that even if the individuals seek or are selected for better performance, we have no guarantee that the system will perform better, the Tragedy of the Commons (Hardin 1968) in which individual self-interest harms collective performance being the classic example of a disconnect between individual adaptation and community failure.[4]

Systems possessing diverse, connected, interacting and adaptive agents often prove capable of producing *emergent* phenomena as well as *complexity*. Before describing complexity, I take a moment to discuss emergence. Emergence refers to higher order structures and functionalities that arise from the interactions of the entities. Ant bridges, market crashes, national cultures, and collective wisdom are all examples of emergence. As the physicist Philip Anderson (1972) wrote in a seminal article, "more is different."

Emergence underpins the idea of the ladder of science. Physics becomes chemistry, chemistry becomes biology, biology becomes psychology, and so on. Or, put another way: cells emerge from the interactions of atoms, organs emerge from the interactions of cells, and societies emerge from the interactions of people. Each level of emergence produces higher order functionalities. Cells divide. Hearts beat. People think. Societies mobilize.

Emergent properties can also be functional. Complex systems often prove robust to internal and external disturbances. This robustness emerges even though it was neither engineered from the top down nor an objective of the parts. Individual species don't set out to create robust ecosystems. Yet, their individual pursuit of survival produces diverse interactions and behaviors that combine to form systems that can withstand mighty blows.

Juxtaposing emergence and complexity provides ample food for thought. Complexity refers to interesting behavior produced by the interactions of simple parts. Emergence refers to simpler higher order behavior that arises from underlying complexity. On the one hand, we have complexity from simplicity. And on the other hand, we have simplicit from complexity.

Keep in mind that complexity can be thought of as a property—something is either complex or not—or it can be conceptualized as a measure: a rainforest can then be said to be more complex than a cornfield. Wolfram (2002) considers complexity to be a matter of kind, a property. He classifies systems as producing one of four types of outcomes that can roughly be characterized as: fixed points, simple structures/periodic orbits, randomness, or complexity. In this conceptualization, complexity lies between simple structures and randomness. Wolfram's definition aligns with casual intuition. Complex outcomes are neither simple patterns nor completely random. They are longer, interesting structures. This approach gives us an exclusionary test for complexity. Complex outcomes are those which cannot be classified as equilibria, simple patterns, or random. This approach works pretty well. Consider the interactions between members of a family. Most family dynamics do not produce fixed points. Families don't do the same thing at every moment. And, though there may be family traditions and the like, there's sufficient novelty that interactions do not produce periodic orbits, where each week mimics the previous one. Despite the novelty, family dynamics probably cannot be considered chaotic. Yes, daily actions may be unpredictable but family life produces recurrent structures and novelty, that is, complexity.

Most categorizations of complexity align with Wolfram's, with complexity residing between order and randomness. Unfortunately, constructing a useful measure of complexity proves difficult (see Lloyd 2001; Mitchell 2009). Measures that sound good in theory often don't work in practice. Let's start with a naïve definition based on description length and move on from there.

Description Length

The most basic definition of description length is simply the number of words required to describe some object, event, or sequence: the more words needed to describe an event, the more complex that event probably is. At the first level of approximation, description length seems to work pretty well. A dead branch is much less complex than a living tree. The branch can be characterized in far fewer words. Similarly, a game of marbles is less complex than a game of soccer. This is true whether we describe the rules or the play of a given game.

A moment's reflection reveals a potential problem with description length: the length depends on the language used. Fortunately, the problem of multiple languages has been overcome. To show how, I have to formalize the notion of minimal description length. It's worth working through this level of detail for two reasons. First, we get a peek at the subtleties involved in constructing a useful definition of complexity. Second, we see the extent to which the complexity depends on the encoding.

First, let me give you an idea of why choice of language matters. Suppose that I want to communicate that a period of human existence had a particular spirit. In the English language, I would have to say something awkward like "the spirit of the age," whereas in German, I could just use the word "zeitgeist."

I can take this same idea and make it more formal. Suppose that I want to describe numbers, but the only number in my language is three. To express the number five, I would have to write $3 + \frac{(3+3)}{3}$. To write six, I would only need to write $3 + 3$. Thus, six would be less complex than five in this language.

To show that the language only matters up to a point, we first need to assume that the phenomenon of interest can be written in a *description language*. We can then define *Kolmogorov complexity* as follows:

Kolmogorov complexity: *The minimum length of a program written in the description language that produces the desired sequence of symbols.*

If we have two languages, A and B, then we can write the Kolmogorov complexity of a sequence s relative to those languages as $K_A(s)$ and $K_B(s)$. The *invariance* result states that given any two languages A and B, there exists some constant C such that for any sequence s, $|K_A(s) - K_B(s)| < C$.[5] This result implies that for sequences with high Kolmogorov complexity, the choice of language does not matter.

So, at this point, we can say that if the thing we're describing is reasonably complex—if it requires a lot of words—then the choice of language doesn't matter much. This does not mean that minimal description length is a perfect measure. It has two serious shortcomings. The first is technical. Given a sequence and an alphabet, there does not necessarily exist an algorithm that will spit out the Kolmogorov complexity.

The second problem is more relevant for our discussion. Description length assigns high values to random sequences. Consider the following three sequences of 0s and 1s. If it helps to make the presentation less abstract, think of 1s as days the stock market goes up and 0s as days that the stock market goes down.

00000000001111111111

01001100011100001111

01101111010110010100

The first sequence can be described as "ten zeroes followed by ten ones." That's a total of six words. The second sequence can be described as "K zeroes then K ones: K from 1 to 4." That's nine words. The third sequence can be described as "zero, two ones, zero, four ones, zero one twice, one, zero, zero one twice, zero zero." That's a lot of words. Yet, if we look at the second and third sequences, we see that the second has patterns and structure and the third is random. Therefore, rather than give a long description of the third, we'd like to just say "it's random." That's only two words.

As the sequences above make clear, description length conflates randomness and complexity. As Huberman and Hogg (1986) point out, complexity is not the same thing as randomness.[6] Instead, complexity lies in between order and disorder. One approach to making randomness less complex which that has been advocated by Murray Gell-Mann and Seth Lloyd, uses the concept of *effective complexity*. This concept emends the idea of minimal description length by considering only the "length of a highly compressed description of its regularities" (Gell-Mann and Lloyd 1996). In other words, Gell-Mann and Lloyd strip away randomness and count only what's left.

Alternatively, complexity can be measured as the difficulty of generating the sequence. This can be calculated either as the minimal number of steps, *logical depth* (Bennet 1988), or as the number of steps in the most plausible sequence of events, *thermodynamic depth* (Lloyd and Pagels 1988). The logical depth of a human being would be huge, but it's relatively small compared to the thermodynamic depth, which also takes into account the most likely evolutionary history that resulted in humans.

Measures that capture the difficulty of generating a phenomenon align with how many people think about complexity, but they too have shortcomings. First, they have computability issues just like description length (Crutchfield and Shalizi 1999). So, the measures work great in theory, but they're cumbersome to apply in practice. A measure that you cannot calculate quickly has limited practical value even if it's theoretically sublime.

A second problem with this whole class of measures is that they apply to a fixed sequence of events or outcomes. The system being studied must have a beginning and an end. We might instead consider a sequence that continues to grow over time and ask how difficult it is to predict that sequence as accurately as possible. This idea underpins Crutchfield and Young's (1989) concept of *statistical complexity*. With statistical complexity, a random sequence would have low complexity because a machine that generates that sequence would be relatively simple. To calculate statistical complexity, an algorithm classifies past data into categories so as to produce patterns that are statistically indistinguishable from the real data. Though not easily calculated, Crutchfield and Young's measure has been derived in some cases.

So What is Complexity?

The analysis so far reveals multiple approaches to measuring complexity. The fact that complexity, which is itself a complex idea, lacks a single definition should, thus, not be a surprise. Nor should it be seen as undermining the science of complexity. A scientific approach to complexity is possible: it just may need multiple lenses. Following Melanie Mitchell

(2009), I see the abundance of definitions as more a strength than a weakness. Diversity can be good. Nevertheless, it would be nice to have at least one or two core definitions, principles, or characteristics of complexity that we can use as a foundation. Here are two: complexity is a BOAR (a somewhat wild one), and complexity is DEEP.

BOAR *Complexity lies* **B**etween **O**rder **A**nd **R**andomness.:

DEEP *Complexity cannot be easily* **D**escribed, **E**volved, **E**ngineered, *or* **P**redicted.

Before moving on, one further point merits attention. Complexity has also been described as lying on the edge of chaos (Langton 1990). I could just wave my hands, claim "chaos = randomness" and move on, but unfortunately, I cannot. Chaos is not randomness. Chaos refers to extreme sensitivity to initial conditions. If we change the initial point by a little bit in a chaotic system, we end up on different paths. Many chaotic systems are completely deterministic. If you know the current state, then you know all future states. When we speak of randomness, we often mean the exact opposite: complete unpredictability. The next flip of the coin does not depend in any way on the current flip of the coin.

There's a simple resolution to this seeming contradiction. Complex systems that produce randomness, such as Wolfram's one-dimensional cellular automata, are also extremely sensitive to initial conditions. They have to be. They're using simple rules, so in order to produce a long random string they have to be adding new information that comes from points far away on the one-dimensional grid. Wolfram (2002) dedicates several pages to this insight in his book. In systems that produce simple structures, there exists very limited sensitivity to initial conditions. Class IV systems (complex systems) lie in between. They produce some sensitivity to initial conditions, but not an extreme amount. So, in a sense, we can say that complexity lies both between order and randomness and between order and chaos. The systems that produce randomness are also highly chaotic.

How can we make sense of all this? Well, we could draw a cover of the *New Yorker* showing Complexistan as a triangle bordered on one side by the Sea of Order, on the second by the Ocean of Chaos, and on the third by the River of Randomness. The interior of that land would not be easily explained. It would be complex.

Complexity and Diversity Together at Last

We can now begin to ask: if complex systems can produce complexity how does diversity contribute to making them do so? I'll begin with a system that's not complex and show that including variation within types and diversity across types doesn't have much of an effect. The setting I want to consider is building a small wooden deck. The process of building a wooden deck is pretty close to an ordered system, and it's not difficult to describe. Once built, the deck will be about as noncomplex as can be. It'll be an equilibrium system with non-adapting parts (save for shrinking and expanding with temperature). But here, we're considering the construction process. The variation in the width of the boards has no functional value. In fact, the builder hopes that whatever variation does exist cancels out due to averaging. Any individual two by four won't be exactly three and a half inches wide (the actual width of a two by four). Some will be a little wider and some a little narrower. With enough boards, these deviations from the mean will cancel one another out—or come close—so that the variation won't matter.

In this example, variation and diversity contribute to complexity, but only a little. The diversity of the parts, the mix of two by four planks, four by four posts, etc. makes the process more complex—in that it makes the structure more elaborate and the process harder to define. But, whether we use BOAR or DEEP, we don't find very much complexity. Overall, then, in noncomplex systems, variation has no real effect, and diversity's effect is minimal.

Now let's move to a system that's more complex: a cakewalk involving nine-year-olds. For those unfamiliar with a cakewalk, imagine the numbers one through twelve written on pieces of tape, which are then stuck to a gym floor, making a circle with a diameter of about eight feet. This creates a clock face. One person stands on each number. When all twelve numbers are covered, the music starts. As in musical chairs, once the music begins the participants walk clockwise around the numbers. When the music stops, each participant stops as well, and a number from one to twelve is drawn from a hat. The participant standing on the number that matches the number drawn wins a cake.

Let's start with a cakewalk with no diversity or variation. Each person walks at exactly the same speed (no variation), and each person moves to the nearest number in front once the music stops (no diversity). Given these assumptions, the cakewalk is not complex. It's not between order and randomness. It's ordered, with a random winner. Nor is it difficult to describe. People walk in a circle. Music stops. A winner is drawn.

Now let's add some variation in walking speed. Some people walk quickly and some people walk slowly. With variation in walking speed, participants bunch up while the music plays. When the music stops, some numbers won't have any people near them, and other numbers will have too many people. If four participants are bunched together near one number, then they will have to scurry to open spots. If they all follow the same rule: *move clockwise to the first open space*, they would all keep circling forward and sequentially fill in the gaps in the circle. If so, depending on the number of fast walkers and how they are spaced, the resulting pattern could be rather beautiful. For instance, suppose eleven fast walkers all bunch up behind a single slow walker. When the music stops, the fast walkers will all walk past the slow walker and one by one peel off onto open numbers. (Think through this pattern; it's pretty cool.)

Next, let's add in some diversity in the behavioral rules, so that when the fast walkers get bunched up they don't necessarily move in an orderly fashion around the circle. Instead, some people might look backward. Others might look across the circle and run toward the first open spot they see. This diversity would destroy order. If the rules people follow are chosen without much thinking, the system will become more random. Again, it won't be entirely random— it will lie *between order and randomness*. As a result, describing the process and predicting where people will end up proves more difficult. The cakewalk becomes DEEP.

Notice the relative magnitude of the effects of variation and diversity. The set of imaginable outcomes in the scenario where we vary walking speed is vastly smaller than the set of outcomes that are possible when we allow diversity in behavioral rules. It will often be the case that when we ramp up the amount of diversity, the set of possible outcomes grows enormous.

To complete the logic, suppose that we have a totally random process, such as throwing a bunch of coins on the floor. If we increase variation by adding coins of different sizes, we don't fundamentally alter the outcomes, which will be random sequences of heads and tails. If we add diversity by adding dice, then we increase the set of possible outcomes. However, we could always convert the numbers on the die using binary notation to heads and tails. If we did, our results would not be any different from the initial experiment. To summarize, increases in variation and diversity can increase complexity but they typically won't have big effects on ordered systems unless they tip them out of the ordered region, or on random systems.

An Example of How Diversity Produces Complexity

To further demonstrate how diversity can produce complexity, I present a model by Nowak and May (1993). This model considers the evolution of cooperation in a spatial setting. In their model, agents play a Prisoners' Dilemma (PD) game. The PD captures a variety of strategic contexts including firm level price competition and arms races. In both cases, each of two players decides whether to cooperate (C) or defect (D). For each player, defecting always gives a higher payoff, but if both players cooperate, they are better off than if they both defect. For example, both firms make higher profits if they keep prices high (if they cooperate), but each does better by cutting prices and getting a bigger market share. The payoffs can be written as follows:

The Prisoners' Dilemma: General Case

Column Player

		C	D
Row Player	C	**R**,R	**S**,T
	D	**T**,S	**P**,P

The payoffs in the PD satisfy two conditions. First, $T > R > P > S$. This condition guarantees that defecting gives the higher payoff regardless of the other player's action. Second, $2R > S + T$. This condition guarantees that joint cooperation produces the highest average payoff. The PD game has been the focus of thousands of papers in fields ranging from economics, to political science, to ecology. It commands so much interest because individual incentives promote defection but collectively everyone is better off cooperating. A numerical example makes these incentives clearer:

The Prisoners' Dilemma: Numerical Example

Column Player

		C	D
Row Player	C	**4**,4	**1**,5
	D	**5**,1	**2**,2

Given the optimality of cooperation, two questions arise. First, can cooperation be induced? Second, will cooperation emerge? By the latter, I mean—will players cooperate even though it is in no one's self-interest to cooperate? In the repeated game setting, individuals play many times in a row. This enables individuals to use more sophisticated strategies. Both questions can be answered in the affirmative. Cooperation can be induced and it also emerges. Consider the strategy called *Tit for Tat*. In *Tit for Tat*, an individual cooperates the first time the game is played and continues to cooperate so long as her opponent cooperates. It's straightforward to see that if both individuals play *Tit for Tat*, then both cooperate. In a famous experiment in which individuals submitted strategies with the goal of earning the highest payoff, *Tit for Tat* proved to be the winning strategy (Axelrod 1984). So, not only can cooperation be supported, it can emerge with real players.

Recall that our focus here is on how diversity can create complexity. In the one-shot PD, there appears to be little complexity—everyone should defect. But suppose that we put a complexity spin on the PD. Recall the core attributes of a complex system: *diverse, interdependent, networked* entities that can *adapt*. By definition, a game assumes interdependent payoffs, and if the initial population includes both defectors and cooperators, then it is diverse. To create a complex system, we need only add dynamics and a network. This is what Nowak and May did. And they did so in the simplest possible way.

Their network was a two-dimensional lattice with N rows and N columns. In other words, they put agents on a checkerboard. Rather than assume that agents play a single agent or the entire population of agents, they assume that each agent plays its four neighbors to the North, South, East, and

West, as shown in the figure below:

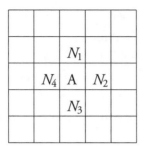

Figure 1.4. Neighbors on a lattice.

To avoid boundary issues, connect the left edge of the lattice to the right edge and the top to the bottom. The first connection creates a tube. The second turns the tube into a donut, what mathematicians call a torus. Many of the canonical models in complex systems take place on tori.

Nowak and May populate their model randomly with cooperators and defectors. They then calculate the *fitness* or *payoff* of each agent as the sum of its payoffs in all four of its games. Consider the following two agents:

	C				D	
C	D	C		C	C	D
	C				D	
	Agent 1				Agent 2	

Using the payoffs from the numerical example of the PD, Agent 1 earns a payoff of twenty, the highest possible payoff, and Agent 2 earns a payoff of only seven (one each in the three games with defectors and four in the game with the cooperator).

To add dynamics to the model, Nowak and May assume that each agent looks to its neighbors. If one of those neighbors gets a higher payoff, then the agent matches the neighbor's action. It's important to note that the agents are not employing sophisticated strategies like *Tit for Tat*. Instead, each agent is either a cooperator or a defector. For the purposes of this discussion, I will refer to the action of an agent as its *type* to align with the earlier definition of diversity of types.

The extended PD can now be thought of as a complex system. It has diverse types with interdependent payoffs situated in a network and we've characterized the dynamics: agents switch their types if one of their neighbors is of a different type and earns a higher payoff. So, what happens? First, note that any agent of the same type as all its neighbors will maintain that type. Therefore, the interior of a region of all cooperators (or defectors) will not change in the next period. What's left to figure out is what happens at the boundary between regions of defectors and cooperators. Surprisingly, defection doesn't necessarily take over. To see why, consider the following configuration:

C	D	C	D	C
D	D	D	D	C
D	D	(D)	D	D
C	C	C	C	D
C	C	C	C	C

Figure 1.5. Evolution of types.

The agent in the center of the grid (denoted by the circle) is of type D. The agent's payoff equals eleven. To determine what the agent's type will be in the next period, we calculate the payoff of each of the agent's neighbors. The neighbors to the East, North, and West all also earn payoffs of eleven, but the neighbor to the South earns a payoff of thirteen. Therefore, in the next period, the agent in the center changes its type to C. This suggests that the system might support cooperation in the long term. And in fact, it can.

The dynamics of this model prove to be complex. They have a long description length, so they are DEEP. And if we apply the BOAR criterion, we see that they are neither ordered nor random. They lie between the two. Early on, the model produces dynamic structures that are consistent with Wolfram's complexity class. Over time, the model produces relatively stable regions of cooperators and defectors with chaotic boundaries (Nowak and May 1992, 1993; Schweitzer et al. 2002). When we have multiple regions, they need not all be in the same state. Some can be fixed, others in periodic orbits, and others chaotically moving about. It makes sense to characterize the overall system as complex.

Emergent Levels: How Simple Parts Create Complex Wholes

In the informal thought experiment of the cakewalk and in the formal PD model, increasing diversity ramps up complexity. These examples align with the common intuition that diversity and complexity go hand in hand. It's natural to think that diversity is required for complexity. Like many intuitive causal relationships, this one proves subtle. A system need not have diverse parts to produce complexity. In fact, two of the most famous complex systems models, Conway's Game of Life and Wolfram's two-dimensional cellular automata model, possess minimal diversity: cells (or agents) assume one of two states—on or off.

Let's consider the Game of Life. As in Nowak and May's PD game, in the Game of Life, agents exist on a torus. Each agent (or cell) can be alive (type 1) or dead (type 0). In the Game of Life, agents have eight neighbors. These include the neighbors to the North, South, East, and West and the four neighbors on the diagonal.

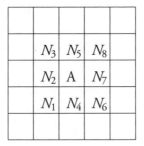

Figure 1.6. Neighbors in the Game of Life.

The rules for the Game of Life are deceptively simple. A dead agent comes to life if it has exactly three live neighbors; otherwise it stays dead. A live agent remains alive if and only if it has two or three live neighbors. Otherwise, it dies, either of boredom (fewer than two live neighbors) or of suffocation (more than three live neighbors). The Game of Life can produce complex patterns including blinkers that flip back and forth, gliders that float across the torus, and even pulsing glider guns that spit out gliders at regular intervals.

If the Game of Life doesn't include much diversity, how can it produce complexity? Two answers: large numbers of parts and interdependence that produces emergent structures. First, the large number answer: a long string of zeros and ones proves a sufficiently rich space to support complexity, just as a long string of DNA can contain the instructions for life. Complexity requires little diversity in the parts, provided there are enough parts. With enough zeros and ones it's possible to say anything. Second, the parts are interdependent. The sum, the component consisting of the parts, can be more complex than the parts themselves. What is a brain but a collection of spatially situated simple parts that interact according to rules? In the brain, the rules depend on chemistry and physics, whereas in the Game of Life, the rules depend on logic, but in both cases simple parts produce complexity.

To see this logic in greater detail, return to the idea of emergence. In the Game of Life, the fundamental objects are networked and interact according to rules. Given that additional structure, the two types can produce higher order structures. Those higher order structures produce the complexity. Let me make this more precise. Even though each agent can be only one of two types, each three by three square of nine cells takes on 512 possible types.[7] Larger configurations of agents can support structures like the aforementioned glider guns. It is those diverse structures that then produce the complexity. Thus, not very diverse fundamental building blocks prove capable of generating complexity because they produce diverse higher order parts.

Here, then, is the take away: *fundamental diversity* is not required for complexity. *Emergent diversity* is. The Game of

Life produces complexity through the interactions of diverse interacting parts, but those parts are not the cells. The relevant parts are the emergent structures, like the gliders. These exist on a higher level. Recall the third type of diversity— community level diversity. Even though the entities themselves are not diverse, they form diverse communities. Just as hydrogen and oxygen can combine to produce water and hydrogen peroxide, live and dead agents can combine to produce blinkers, gliders, and glider guns.

In characterizing the relationship between diversity and complexity, it is also important to remember that diversity is not sufficient on its own to produce complexity. If you visit a landfill, you'll see diverse consumer waste products, but you won't see much complexity. That's because pieces of trash don't interact in interesting ways. As the saying goes: when you put garbage in, you cannot get anything but garbage out. At the same time, a system cannot just have any interacting rules and produce complexity. The rules must interact in particular ways. Flip open your computer and write a computer model with a large number of types of agents. Make each of those types meaningfully diverse; that is assign each a distinct behavioral rule. When you're finished, you're more likely to get a mangle, stasis, or randomness than complexity.

For some classes of models, it has been shown that in the space of all possible interacting rules, complexity is a low probability event (Wolfram 2002). Creating a complex system from scratch takes skill (or evolution). Therefore, when we see diverse complex systems in the real world, we should not assume that they've been assembled from whole cloth. Far more likely, they've been constructed bit by bit.

Each step along the way, complex systems rely on their rule-based parts to adapt to changing surroundings. London began with a few individuals carving out a life along a bend in the river. Over time, as London expanded, the parts—people, businesses, governments, and social organizations—adapted. In turn, they enabled ever more diversity to emerge and the city to become ever more complex.

Measuring the Effects of Diversity in Complex Systems

I've shown some examples in which diversity helps produce of complexity. Later in the book, I'll focus on the effects of complexity. That analysis will be made more difficult because complex systems are assembled through selection. Only entities that function well within the system survive. This process of selection of the entities in a complex system can be thought of as a form of assembly. By that I mean, the system does not contain agents with foresight or intention who put the pieces in place. Ecosystems self-assemble. Other systems, such as organizations, are assembled deliberately with a specific purpose in mind. Market economies and political systems lie in between. They self-assemble to some extent, and they're also partly assembled. In social system, actors—governments and other large organizations—structure interactions and incentives so as to alter the assembly process.

Assembly implies that the level of diversity in a system has survived some winnowing process. This winnowing creates three problems for empirical tests of the effects of diversity. I refer to these as the *problem of multiple causes, the sample problem*, and *selection (squared) bias*. I cover each in turn.

The Problem of Multiple Causes

In most complex systems, multiple factors influence the independent variable of interest. Economic growth, ecosystem robustness, etc. depend on more than one variable. We cannot therefore just run a regression of economic growth on human diversity or of robustness on the diversity of flora and fauna. We must also account for other variables. Determining the independent effect of diversity may be problematic because the independent variables may not be sufficiently random.

An example makes this clearer. Suppose that the social networks that survive can be classified as one of two types. The first type consists of diverse people with few connections, and the second type consists of homogeneous people who have lots of connections.[8] To ground the analysis, suppose that networks of the first type prove to be more innovative. We cannot discern whether that innovativeness was due to the diversity of the individuals in the network or to the looseness of their connections. To unpack the true cause, we would also need either strongly connected networks of diverse people or weakly connected networks of homogeneous people. Those might not exist. Thus, we might not be able to determine the effect of diversity.

Therefore, stylized facts that more diverse societies are more innovative or less trusting do not necessarily imply that diversity causes those phenomena (Putnam 2007). The effect (innovation or trust) might be caused by lower connectivity between people or by something else. If diversity correlates with some other characteristic of systems, we cannot be certain whether an empirical phenomenon is caused by diversity, the other characteristic, or some combination of the two.

The Sample Problem

The second difficulty for empirical analysis concerns defining the sample. Do we take all possible combinations of entities or only those that have survived some form of selection? Consider recipes. Recipes exist in a complex system. They adapt to tastes (or more accurately, they're adapted). And they face selective pressure. If a recipe's no good, it won't survive. The idea that recipes evolve is supported by data. Physicists who examined cookbooks from four cultures found a scale-invariant distribution of ingredients that's consistent with a "mutate and copy" model of recipe evolution in which new recipes make small modifications in existing recipes (Kinouchi et al. 2008).

The recipes that we find in books, then, are not random combinations of ingredients. They're the result of a long process of combining and winnowing. To see why this causes a problem for empirical research, suppose that we want to learn whether a greater diversity of ingredients improves the quality of the recipe. Making this a well-defined problem requires measures of diversity and quality. Let's use the number of ingredients as a diversity measure. To measure quality, assume that there exists a panel of food tasters who rate each dish between one and ten.

Here's the key question: how do we define the sample? Over what set of recipes do we test whether quality improves with diversity? Do we consider all possible recipes? Do we consider only those recipes that currently exist? Or do we attempt to define a set of theoretically plausible recipes and randomly select from that distribution? If I choose all recipes, then I will find that quality decreases with higher diversity.

Diversity does not always increase quality within this domain. An arbitrary combination of ingredients probably produces an inedible mélange. Peanut butter-watermelon-squash enchiladas drenched in chocolate sauce doesn't sound tasty.

Selection (Squared) Bias

Suppose that we define our sample to be those recipes whose qualities lie above some survivability threshold—perhaps recipes that appear in a cookbook. This selection could bias empirical tests. For example, suppose that recipes with more ingredients require more time and effort. If the person writing the cookbook assumed that people trade off the quality of a recipe against the costs of making it, then the author would place a higher quality bar on recipes with more ingredients. A mediocre recipe with two ingredients might make the book, but a mediocre recipe with twenty ingredients wouldn't. However, a great recipe with lots of ingredients would be included. With this rule of thumb for choosing recipes, the result would be a collection whose quality would improve with diversity.

Let me put numbers to this logic to make it more precise. Assume recipes have qualities between zero and twenty and that the cookbook's author requires a quality greater than or equal to the number of ingredients to include the recipe in the book. If so, recipes with two ingredients will have qualities between two and twenty, recipes with five ingredients will have qualities between five and twenty, and recipes with fifteen ingredients will have qualities between fifteen and twenty. An empirical test that regresses the quality of a recipe on the number of ingredients will find that quality increases with the number of ingredients.

Notice that diversity itself isn't producing any benefits. The cookbook writer's recipe filter, and not any direct benefit from diversity, causes the diverse recipes to be better. This creates what statisticians call *selection bias*: the cases considered aren't random. In complex systems, (statistical) selection bias is caused by (evolutionary) selective pressures. The species that currently exist in the world have survived selective pressures. Therefore, the selection (the set of species existing in an ecosystem) may be biased by evolutionary selective pressures. We can think of this as selection bias caused by selection or *selection (squared) bias*. If a system exhibits selection (squared) bias, diversity may appear beneficial but not be.

Example: The Diversity-Stability Debate

As mentioned in the prelude to this book, in ecology there exists what is called the diversity-stability debate. This debate focuses on whether diverse ecosystems are more dynamically stable and more robust to perturbations. Later, I flesh out the distinction between stability and robustness in more detail. For now, think of a stable ecosystem as one that will go back to its equilibrium if the sizes of the populations are changed, and a robust ecosystem as one that can survive environmental shifts and the loss or addition of a species.

The diversity-stability debate demonstrates how the selection (squared) bias plays out in a real world example. The ecosystems we study aren't random. They've been chosen by evolution. The debate may also exhibit the problem of multiple causes if diverse ecosystems differ systematically from nondiverse ecosystems. That this basic of a question—does diversity make ecosystems more stable and more robust?—has proven difficult to prove empirically or theoretically speaks to the challenges of making definitive statements about the effects of diversity in complex systems.

This diversity-stability debate has current relevance given recent declines in the number of species. If species reductions create less stable ecosystems, then current reductions could beget future reductions and even collapses.[9]

The origins of the diversity-stability debate are empirical, but theory also plays a central role. A nonspecialist reading of the literature suggests that early on most ecologists accepted that ecosystem stability and robustness increased with species diversity. The evidence for this came first from the extremes. Rainforests were relatively stable while farms at times suffer from massive infestations and blights. Furthermore, islands with fewer species were more susceptible to invasion (Odum 1953; Elton 1958). (Bracket for the moment that rainforests have been constructed through tens of thousands of years of evolution while farms are artificially constructed.) The observation that rainforests were less prone to booms and busts led to the hypothesis that having multiple predators and prey made a system less likely to have large population fluctuations.

The logic for why diversity increased stability, as advanced by MacArthur (1955), goes as follows. If you have a single predator and its population declines, then its prey's population might explode. If swallows are the only check on mosquitos, then a sudden decline in swallows for some external reason will result in giant swarms of mosquitos. If, however, bats are also present in the ecosystem, a decline in swallows will be offset by an increase in the number of bats, thus preventing the mosquito population from getting too large.

This logic seems pretty compelling, yet it wasn't completely accepted. Part of the reason for the lack of acceptance had to do with the distinction between stability and robustness. And part had to do with the fact that the empirical evidence is messy (Woodwell and Smith 1969).

Robert May (1973) complicated the debate by constructing a mathematical model that showed the opposite conclusion, causing quite a stir. In May's model, interactions between species were assigned randomly. May found that increasing the number of species and the number of connections led to lower asymptotic stability. In retrospect, this result isn't as devastating to the MacArthur model as was first thought. In real ecosystems, interaction strengths evolve. This means that that what we see in the real world isn't a random collection. Think back to the discussion of random and assembled recipes. There the assembled recipes showed increased quality in the number of ingredients, but that would not be true for random recipes. From one perspective then, we should not be surprised that randomly created ecosystems are less stable. If we just started dumping species of all kinds into a habitat, we'd likely get an initial maelstrom, in which many species swirled to their deaths.

One response to May's result has been to replicate it with more realistic assumptions on interaction strengths. Yodzis (1981) constructed models with interaction strengths calibrated to real ecosystem data. He found that these models produce more complex *and* more stable dynamics than did

May's random interaction strengths model. This does not settle the debate so much as open more questions. Additional theoretical and empirical research has further muddied the waters. Tilman (1997) and others have constructed ecosystems in prairies and have explored how those ecosystems have fared over time. They have found a strong correlation between diversity and robustness.[10] Note that here, I use the term robustness because Tilman and his colleagues examined whether the ecosystems continue to function and not whether they return to the same equilibrium.

In his excellent book on ecological commons problems, Levin (2000) describes how May's results have been misinterpreted. Recall that May focuses on asymptotic stability. Stability and robustness differ. A system could be unstable, or continue to fluctuate, yet be very robust. Levin points to viruses. The flu virus never reaches an asymptotic equilibrium. Were it to, we could eradicate it with a vaccine. Viruses' robustness stems from the fact that they present a moving target. We're not fighting a flu virus, we're fighting a diverse, fluctuating population of flu viruses.

Schneider and Kay (1994) offer a similar critique. They view the entire debate as misguided. Diversity, they argue, could be counted in many ways. Do we use number of species? Do we count the millions of bacteria in the soil? It's difficult to make an empirical claim without a well-defined independent variable. Furthermore, they argue, stability doesn't make any sense. Here they echo Levin by noting that ecosystems are continuously in flux. Given that ecosystems are complex adaptive systems, Schneider and Kay fail to see how it makes much sense to talk about diversity creating stability when the systems being studied are not stable.

The deep unanswered question in this entire debate is why are systems diverse. Later in this book, I'll discuss how diversity contributes to robustness through particular functions. But I don't answer why robustness, a system level property, emerges in ecosystems. In designed systems, such as political systems or traffic systems, one can make an argument that the designers are mindful of robustness in their planning, that robustness can be built into a system (Bednar 2009). I agree that this is possible and only add that designers often borrow features from robust ecosystems even though the origins or emergence of those features within ecosystems remains somewhat of a mystery.

2

MEASURING DIVERSITY

> I often say that when you can measure what you are
> speaking about, and express it in numbers, you know
> something about it; but when you cannot measure it,
> when you cannot express it in numbers, your knowledge
> is of a meager and unsatisfactory kind.
>
> —LORD KELVIN

To move beyond loose, informal characterizations of diversity requires formal measures. Without measures, we can at best make qualitative comparisons.[11] Any foray into measures obliges the reader to acquire notation, definitions, and subtle distinctions that may lack immediate context and lends an austerity to the text, but so be it. My intent is not to discourage all but the most persistent readers, but to build a common vocabulary and basis of knowledge.

Counting the number of types is the most obvious way to measure diversity. Ecologists refer to this as *species richness.* Types, though, may not be well defined, a point I return to later. Often, we'll be interested in the distribution across the types or the relative sizes of those types. Economists are interested less in the number of firms in a market than in their market shares. And ecologists care as much about *species abundance*, the distribution of species' population sizes, as they do about the number of species. Therefore, we need to do more than count the number of types, so we need multiple measures of diversity.

Over the past half-century, statisticians, ecologists, computer scientists, and economists have proposed a variety of diversity measures. In what follows, I differentiate among five types of measures: *variation, entropy, distance, attribute*, and *population measures*. These five types of measures can be placed in the three categories described earlier.

- **Diversity within a Type:** *Variation*
- **Diversity across Types:** *Entropy, Distance, Attribute*
- **Diversity of Community Composition:** *Population*

Before diving into notation and definitions, I make three observations about measures in general and diversity measures in particular. First, measures can be constructed from the ground up by experimenting with mathematical formulae, or they can be derived analytically from a list of desiderata. Though the latter approach might appear more scientific, in practice the two approaches prove more alike than different. Most intuitive measures can be shown to satisfy desirable axioms. If they didn't, the measures wouldn't make sense or function empirically.[12]

Second, diversity measures compress information. They transform populations of diverse entities into single numbers. In the process, meaningful distinctions disappear: information gets lost in the translation. For each of the measures I describe, with a little mathematical effort anyone can construct populations that differ substantially yet yield the same diversity value. For example, you might show that the diversity of Microsoft Word fonts equals the diversity of deciduous trees in Ohio. This may seem like a goofy exercise, but such calculations reveal a cost of information compression. A regression that uses diversity as an independent variable treats fonts and trees identically. Ecologists seeking empirical relationships between diversity and some functional characteristic like ecosystem robustness, therefore, cannot help but place radically different ecosystems in the same box.

Finally, diversity measures can be applied to cultures, languages, makes of automobiles, ecosystems, and even toothbrushes. Each of these sets of types has distinct properties. One size can't fit all, owing to the relationships between entities. For example, bird species have genetic lineages. Measures of bird diversity can exploit that branching structure. Those same measures may not work for breakfast cereals, which lack genetic history, and therefore cannot be arranged in a branching network. This is not to deny that one could identify some parental lineages in cereal, such as when Corn Flakes begat Frosted Flakes. But, unlike birds, new cereals can arise without having parents. Thus, we will need more than one measure.

The multiplicity of measures allows us to pick the one that fits the context. It also gives us multiple lenses to view the same data, adding to our collective understanding. Stirling (2007) shows how these lenses are related, how they can be placed within a general framework.

The first type of measure, *variation measures*, should be familiar to most readers. These measures capture diversity along a single numerical attribute such as beak length or income within a type. The most common measures of this type are *variance* and its square root, *standard deviation*.

The second type of measure, *entropy measures*, capture distributions across types. These measures often depend on both the number of types and the evenness of the distribution across those types. A basket with ten oranges, ten apples, and ten bananas would be thought by most people to be more diverse than a basket with twenty-nine apples and one orange. Entropy measures capture the fact that the first basket has more types (three to two) and that its distribution across those types is more even. Entropy measures come from a specific family of measures. By changing a single parameter, we can vary the weight that an entropy measure places on the number of types relative to the weight it places on the distribution across those types. In the formal construction that follows, the parameter α equals the power to which the probabilities of the different types are raised. Thus when $\alpha = 0$ the measure equals the number of types.

Entropy measures also have the property that sets containing equal numbers of N types have an entropy equal to N. Within the family of generalized entropy measures, one particular measure known as Shannon's entropy (the limit as α approaches 1) satisfies a list of desiderata one might compile for a diversity measure. For this reason, ecologists, computer scientists, information scientists, physicists, and some economists use Shannon's measure. A downside to Shannon's entropy is that it requires the use of logarithms which are neither easy to compute nor intuitive. For that reason, a diversity measure with $\alpha=2$ may be the most commonly used measure. This measure has various names—as discussed below—depending on the discipline. In each of these disciplines, the diversity measure serves as a benchmark for more nuanced analysis. For example, studies of political competition consider the ideological breadth of the parties as well as their effective number (Grzymala-Busse 2007).

For all their benefits, entropy measures have what some see as a large flaw. They do not take into account the extent of the differences between the types. The entropy of a basket with ten apples, ten bananas, and ten oranges exceeds the entropy of a basket with eleven apples, ten iguanas, and nine orchids because the first basket has a more even distribution. Entropy measures don't capture the fact that iguanas and orchids differ from apples much more than do oranges and bananas. As difficult as comparing apples and oranges may be, comparing oranges and iguanas must be even harder. And for that reason, two types of measures have been constructed that take type level differences into account.

The first type of measure that takes into account differences I'll call *distance measures*. One measure, due to Weitzman (1992), assumes a preexisting *distance function* for pairs of types. If we use color, growing region, and how they're consumed, the distance between an apple and an orange equals three: they differ in color, in the regions in which they grow, and in whether they must be peeled. Using these dimensions, the distance between an orange and a banana would equal two. To calculate the distance between an iguana and an orange, we would need more dimensions. That distance, by the way, would be pretty large, certainly bigger than two. For some classes of types, distance functions exist in the literature and have wide acceptance. As mentioned, in biological contexts, distance can be measured phylogenetically. For other classes of types, such as human minds or art, no natural distance function may exist.

Given a distance function, a naive way to measure diversity would be to be to add up all of the distances between the members of the set. This approach has several flaws. Most notably, it would increase diversity whenever types are added to the set. A set containing ten apples and one orange would have a total distance between all types equal to ten times two (the distance from an apple to an orange), or twenty. Adding an eleventh apple wouldn't make the set more diverse, yet it would increase the total distance to twenty-two.

The second approach that takes into account type level differences relies on attributes. These *attribute measures* identify the attributes of each type in the set and then count up the total number of unique attributes. In some cases, the number of distinct attributes captures diversity better than does the number of types. Imagine a geeky professor sporting a pocket protector containing four pens: two blue pens with blue caps and two red pens with red caps. The set of two copies of two pens has a type diversity of two. Suppose that the professor mistakenly places a red cap on a blue pen and vice versa. Now he has four unique pens, which has diversity equal to four. Diversity has increased. Yet has it? If we instead count the attributes: two red pen bases, two blue pen bases, two red caps, and two blue caps, the diversity equals four regardless of the assignment of caps to bases.

The final type of diversity measure considers *disjoint populations*. These measures capture differences between sets of types, whereas all of the previous measures consider the diversity of a single set. Population measures enable scientists to determine changes in composition. These measures can capture sensitivity to initial conditions, path dependence, and the stochasticity of processes.

What is a Type?

Before digging into the definitions, I digress a moment on the notion of a type. In thinking about types, a good place to start is with the distinction between *taxonomies* and *typologies*. A taxonomy classifies objects or things based on a hierarchy. In biology, linguistics, and other fields, origins determine that hierarchy. A typology classifies those same things by their attributes. A taxonomic classification of English words places words borrowed from French near each other, whereas a typological classification places nouns with nouns and adjectives with adjectives. A biologist who studies birds might specialize on related species. This would be a taxonomic approach. Or, that biologist might study all birds found in a particular area. That would be a typologic approach.

Prior to researching this book, I incorrectly assumed that taxonomic and feature-based typological classifications of species would be nearly identical, that if two butterflies looked identical they would be genetically identical. That's not true. A good number of species of snakes, birds, and salamanders possess similar attributes but have distinct phylogenies. Biologists refer to these as *cryptic species*.

Species are a kind of type, and as is true for most types, the boundaries of species become blurry. For example, a plunge into the biology literature reveals notions of species to be contested on several fronts. Textbooks in biology define a species as a population or set of populations capable of interbreeding and producing fertile offspring. So, for example, the cardinal population in my backyard in Ann

Arbor, Michigan, belongs to the same species as cardinals that reside in Madison, Wisconsin, even though they belong to two separate populations. This basic definition, which was put forth by Ernst Mayr over a half-century ago, (de Queiroz 2005), leaves some wiggle room for interpretation and second-guessing.[13]

Characterizing the equivalent of species in the worlds of products and ideas is even more problematic. What constitutes a "species," or type, in the world of ideas is determined through decentralized processes involving historians, marketers, artists, patent lawyers, and governments. It's accurate to say that types are socially constructed, politically constructed, and economically constructed.

Nowhere is social construction more widespread than in the typing of humans. Consider the notion of race. Standard categories of race do not match one to one with genetics. Even more troubling, self-reported conceptions of race often differ from the races that people internally feel themselves to be, and from the races that others perceive them to be (Harris 2004). And, even if we were to buy into the notion that there are, say, five races, how do we count multiracial people? Do we count each unique fractional representation of races as a separate new race? Or do we count all multiracial people as a sixth race and systematically understate the diversity of a population?

Moving back to the more general discussion of what is a type, it is probably not too much of a reach to say that the definition of types depends upon the question being asked. A candy store that sells thousands of types of candy can be thought of as selling either one type of good—candy—or, if we distinguish among the many brands and varieties, thousands of types. Whether we differentiate between a Clark

Bar and a Butterfinger depends on whether we're interested in the diversity of individual choices (in which case we do) or how economic diversity drives macro-economic growth (in which case we do not).

To take another example, in classifying the afternoon sky, weather reports use words like cloudy, partly cloudy, and clear. Detailed meteorological analyses of weather patterns classify clouds as cirrus, cumulus, or stratus, with subcategories within those broader classifications such as cumulonimbus (big thunderheads) and cirrocumulus (small cotton balls) (Hamblyn 2001).

Many common categories, like the cloud categories, are based on exemplars. When someone mentions the word "muffin," our minds invoke a typical instantiation of a muffin. And we tend to identify other things as muffins if they are similar to the image we invoked. If we are asked about a chair, child's wagon, or glass of water, we do not think of attributes: "*chair*: supporting structure (usually four legs), seat, and a back (typically); *child's wagon*: red, metal, four-wheeled vehicle of length three feet and height eighteen inches with sides but not a top, and a handle; *glass of water*: collection of molecules containing two hydrogen atoms and one oxygen atom at a temperature between zero and one hundred degrees Celsius." Instead, we picture in our mind a prototypical chair, wagon, or glass of water.

Our preferences often drive our categorizations. What matters to each of us differs. Thus, we differ in what we consider to be a type. One person's piece of tile is another person's green, Pewabic, craftsman tile. Furthermore, the less consensus on the functional consequences, the more likely that we will disagree on the set of types. People who love meat classify cuts of beef by their location on the steer. People on diets may classify those same cuts of meat by how many calories they have per ounce. And, people on tight budgets classify them by price per pound. Here, diversity of preferences begets diversity of types.

Type classifications also depend on expertise. All else equal, the more experience or interest we have in a particular area, the greater our ability to refine the set of types. A typical middle-aged American may classify music into six types: rap, jazz, classical, rock, blues, and folk. A musician may have upwards of twenty classifications for jazz alone. If asked about a dresser, many people might think of two prototypes: a tall four- or five-drawer dresser and a shorter, wider dresser with two sets of drawers and perhaps a mirror. A furniture designer will invoke many more prototypes based on style, era, and function.

These caveats aside, I will now describe formal measures of diversity. From here on, I consider how types form rather than engage in semantics over what is a type. I try to avoid subtleties and choose categories with rather thick boundaries— I'll say that phones differ from tennis shoes and game theory differs from poetry—but I won't dare to tread on the question of types of music or novels or sofa beds.

Measures of Diversity

It is now time to introduce formal definitions. In what follows, I rely on the following notation:

$i \in \{1, 2, \ldots, N\}$ *denotes the* **types** *in the population.*

m_i denotes the **number of type** in the population. The total
population is of size $M = \sum_{i=1}^{N} m_i$.

$p_i = \frac{m_i}{M}$ denotes i's **proportion** in the population.

$d(i, j)$ denotes the **distance** between type i and j.

$a \in \{1, \ldots, A\}$ denotes the **attributes** in the population.

Throughout, I assume proportions with respect to number
and not some other measure, such as biomass or cost. I do
this for expository clarity, not because it always makes sense
to do so. When computing the diversity of an ecosystem,
proportion of biomass has greater relevance. The number
of termites can vastly exceed the number of elephants yet
have approximately the same biomass. Energy can also be
a good measure. Energy and biomass differ by an amount
that depends on species size. Energy used by an animal
scales to the three-fourths power of body mass. A male
elephant weighs around 10,000 pounds. This means that
the energy used by that elephant would be proportional
to one-tenth of its body mass. Similarly, a barn owl that
weighs a pound would use energy proportional to its weight,
and a mouse, which weighs one-twentieth of pound, would
use energy proportional to twice its weight.[14] Thus, 10,000
pounds of owls use ten times the energy of an elephant, and
10,000 pounds of mice use twenty times the energy of an
elephant.

Variation Measures

The first type of measures, *variation measures*, apply to differences in measurements of an attribute within a given type.

Variation measures receive substantial coverage in statistics textbooks, so I offer only a brief treatment here. Variation is measured within a population. That population might be elephant seals, and the attribute under consideration could be their flippers or brains. Within the population of elephant seals, flipper sizes and brain sizes vary.

To capture variation, statisticians rely on two related measures: *variance* and the *coefficient of variation*.[15]

Measures of Variation

Let $x_1, x_2, \ldots, x_m$ denote the values of an attribute among the members of a type. Let $\mu = \frac{1}{m}(x_1 + x_2 + \cdots + x_m)$ equal the mean of the attribute values.

The **variance** of the values, σ^2, equals the average squared distance from a point to the mean:

$$\sigma^2 = \sum_{i=1}^{m} \frac{(x_i - \mu)^2}{m}.$$

The **coefficient of variation** equals the square root of the variance (the **standard deviation**) divided by the mean:

$$c_v = \frac{\sigma}{\mu}.$$

Though these measures have similar forms, they differ in how they characterize maximal diversity. To maximize variance, values must be bunched at the extremes. To maximize the coefficient of variation, the mean must be small. Thus, if one attribute has a high value and all the others have low values, the coefficient of variation will be large.[16] The coefficient of variation measure does not satisfy symmetry: if one variable has a low value and the rest have high values, the coefficient takes on a relatively low value because the mean is high.

These technical details become relevant when applying these measures to a particular domain (Harrison and Klein 2007). Consider the claim that increasing the variation in attribute values makes a population better able to adapt to a changing environment. That claim would hold as the population moved from low variation (all attribute values the same) to moderate variation (many distinct attribute values), but it probably would not hold as variation increased from moderate to maximal. Recall that the distribution that maximizes variation implies only extreme values. Successful adaptation probably requires a distribution that includes intermediate values as well.

Entropy Measures

Entropy measures consider the number of types and the distribution across those types. Entropy measures map probability distributions over types into real numbers. To describe entropy measures, I begin by describing three desiderata, written as axioms, that we might want a diversity measure to satisfy. It can be shown that Shannon's entropy uniquely satisfies those desiderata among continuous functions. I then describe a family of entropy measures indexed by a single parameter for which Shannon's entropy, as well as several other common measures, are special cases.[17] By convention, entropy measures are written H_N, where N denotes the number of types.

The first desideratum states that the measure satisfy a *symmetry* condition on proportions, that is, the diversity of the proportions $(0.3, 0.4, 0.3)$ should be equal to the diversity of the proportions $(0.4, 0.3, 0.3)$. In other words, it does not matter which type is in which proportion. A basket with six apples and five oranges has the same entropy as a basket with five apples and six oranges.

Symmetry: *The value of the function H_N does not change if the types are renumbered; i.e., $H_N(p_1, p_2, \ldots, p_N) = H_N(p_2, p_1, \ldots, p_N)$.*

The second desideratum says that diversity is maximized when types exist in equal proportions.

Maximum at Equality: *The function H_N is maximized for N types when $p_i = \frac{1}{N}$ for all i.*

The third desideratum applies to decompositions of types into subtypes. Consider a set containing three types of flora and two types of fauna. We could compute the diversity over all five types—*total diversity.* We could compute diversity at the level of flora and fauna—*between category diversity.* We could also compute the diversity within the flora and fauna categories—*within category diversity.* The third desideratum requires that total diversity equals between category diversity plus within category diversity. Writing this formally requires additional notation. Let K denote the number of categories, and B the number of types within each category.[18]

Decomposability: *Assume N types that can be placed in K categories, each containing B types (note: $N = B \cdot K$). Denote the probability of category j by q_j and the probability of each type by $p_{j\ell}$, where j denotes its category and ℓ the type within that category. The functions H_N, H_K, and H_B satisfy*

$$H_N(p_{11}, p_{12}, p_{1B}, \ldots, p_{KB}) = H_K(q_1, q_2, \ldots, q_K)$$

$$+ \sum_{i=1}^{K} q_k H_B \left(\frac{p_{k1}}{q_k}, \frac{p_{k2}}{q_k}, \ldots, \frac{p_{kB}}{q_k} \right)$$

The *Entropy theorem* states that a unique functional form, up to parameter choices, satisfies these three desiderata.

The Entropy Theorem

Any continuous function that satisfies **symmetry**, **maximum at equality**, and **decomposability** has the following functional form:

$$H_N(p_1, p_2, \ldots, p_N) = -C \sum_{i=1}^{N} p_i \log_b(p_i),$$

where C is a positive constant and b equals the base of the logarithm. When $C = 1$ and $b = 2$, the formula gives **information entropy**.

The entropy measures belong to a larger class known as *generalized entropy functions*. The class also contains more intuitive and easily calculated functions.

Generalized Entropy Functions

The class of **generalized entropy functions** can be written as follows:

$$G_N^\alpha(p_1, p_2, \ldots, p_N) = \left(\sum_{i=1}^{N} p_i^\alpha \right)^{\frac{1}{1-\alpha}}.$$

The following are special cases:

Number of Types ($\alpha = 0$):

$$G_N^0(p_1, p_2, \ldots, p_N) = N$$

Diversity Index ($\alpha = 2$):

$$G_N^2(p_1, p_2, \ldots, p_N) = \left(\sum_{i=1}^{N} p_i^2 \right)^{-1}$$

Most Abundant Type ($\alpha \to \infty$):

$$G_N^\infty(p_1, p_2, \ldots, p_N) = \frac{1}{p^*}, \quad \text{where } p^* = \max_i p_i$$

Shannon Entropy ($\alpha \to 1$):

$$G_N^\alpha(p_1, p_2, \ldots, p_N) = -C \sum_{i=1}^{N} p_i \log_e(p_i)$$

Notice that for every generalized entropy function, the entropy of an equal distribution across the number of types equals the number of types:

$$G_N^\alpha \left(\frac{1}{N}, \frac{1}{N}, \ldots, \frac{1}{N} \right) = N.$$

The simplest entropy measure is the number of types ($\alpha = 0$). Unfortunately, the number of types does not capture what people often mean by diversity. The distribution across the types also matters. A group with ten men and ten women has more gender diversity than a group with nineteen men and one woman.

The case $\alpha = 2$, what I will call the **diversity index**, is the most common measure of diversity. This measure, or its inverse, appears in the literature under various names: *Herfindahl index* (economics), *effective number of parties* (political science), and (almost) *Simpson's index* (ecology).[19]

Comparing functions within the class of generalized entropy functions can help give intuition for what Shannon entropy captures. For large α, generalized entropy places relatively more weight on the more probable types. In the limit as α approaches infinity, it places all of the weight on the most probable type. For α equals two, the measure weights proportions by their proportions. By that I mean that it multiplies proportion p_i by itself. As a result, the inverse of the diversity index equals the probability that two randomly selected members of the population will be of the same type.[20] For α approaching zero, the entropy measure counts the types. Shannon entropy corresponds to the limit as α approaches one, so we can infer that Shannon entropy places slightly more than proportional weight on unlikely outcomes and slightly less than proportional weight on likely outcomes.

Distance Measures

As already mentioned, entropy measures fail to take into account the extent of differences between the types. In contemplating ecosystem preservation and regeneration, differences between the types may be more important than differences in the distribution across the types. Consider a crude model of an ecosystem with multiple species at each of several trophic levels. (For nonbiologists, a species' trophic level refers to its place in the food chain: what it eats and what eats it. Two species reside at the same trophic level if they eat the same things and are eaten by the same things.) Ecosystem preservation requires maintaining at least one species at each trophic level. Otherwise, some species have nothing to eat. Assuming species at the same trophic level exhibit similar characteristics, a diversity measure that takes into account distances between attributes of species would find greater diversity in ecosystems with more trophic levels.

I next present a diversity measure proposed by Weitzman (1992). This measure is designed to capture diversity in terms of distance. You can think of all of the entities connected in a giant network and the distance between two entities as how many links (branches) you must traverse to get from one to the other. Here, I restrict the domain to types arranged in a rooted tree network. Weitzman's measure applies more generally but, in effect, it always creates a rooted tree. For ease of presentation, I assume the types lie at the ends of branches in the network. The network has $L + 1$ levels, with the ends of the branches being level 0 and the root being level L. For a given type, define its *ancestors* to be all nodes that lie above it in the network. In the Figure 2.1, I show a four-level network and denote the ancestors of type a with solid dots.

The distance between type a and type c equals the *lowest level* at which a and c have a common ancestor. In the example above, that distance equals two.

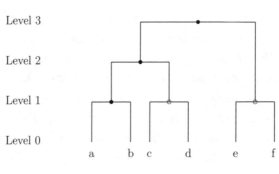

Figure 2.1. (levels).

Weitzman Diversity

The **Weitzman diversity**, $W(S)$, of a of set of types given a distance function $d(i, j)$ is constructed recursively as follows:

- **Step 1:** Let S equal the empty set and set $W(S) = 0$
- **Step 2:** Randomly choose a type to add to S
- **Step 3:** Choose a type j of least distance to a member of S according to $d(\cdot, \cdot)$

  – Increase $W(S)$ by the distance from j to S
  – Add type j to the set S

- **Step 4:** If not all types belong to S go to **Step 2**

To compute the Weitzman diversity in the example given in the previous figure with levels 0 through 3, the algorithm begins with a random type, a, and sets W equal to zero. The set S, therefore, equals the singleton $\{a\}$. The algorithm then chooses the type closest to a, which is b, increments W by

$d(a, b) = 1$, and adds b to the set S. The algorithm then chooses a type closest to the set $S = \{a, b\}$. This type could be either c or d. The distance from either c or d to each member of S equals two, so W increases to 3. Suppose that the next type chosen is c. The diversity of the set S can be written as $W(a, b, c) = 3$. Next, the algorithm chooses d. Its distance to the set S equals one (its distance to c), so $W(a, b, c, d) = 4$. Next, e (or f) is added, and its distance to S equals 3. Finally, f is added to the set. Its distance to the set equals one, because $d(e, f) = 1$. Therefore, the Weitzman diversity of the set, $W(\{a, b, c, d, e, f\})$, equals eight.

Weitzman diversity has several nice properties. The measure can capture the impact of type or species loss. The decrease in diversity from a loss of a single type equals the least distance from that type to some other type. Loss of a type that differs significantly from other types, such as a species that occupies its own trophic level, results in a large loss of diversity. A similar logic implies that the time required to reproduce a lost species through mutation correlates with distance in the tree. Species that branched off earlier would be more difficult to reproduce.

Alas, the measure is not perfect. In some cases, no natural distance measure between the types may exist. In that case, Weitzman diversity cannot be computed. In other cases, a graph of the set of distances may not produce a network that looks like a tree. In the latter cases, Weitzman diversity can still be calculated, but its value need not be unique.[21]

Attribute Measures

As an alternative to Weitzman diversity, several scholars have proposed diversity measures based on attributes. The simplest measure, what I call *attribute diversity*, adds up the number of unique attributes represented in the population. The formula weights all attributes equally. Some attributes, such as the ability to fly, may be more valuable than others. To capture variations in importance of attributes, the *weighted attribute diversity measure* allows for individual weights to be assigned to the attributes.

Attribute Diversity

The **Attribute Diversity**, $\mathcal{A}$, of a set S equals the number of distinct attributes present in the population of types.

Given a type i, let $A(i)$ denote the attributes expressed by type i:

$$\mathcal{A}(S) = \left| \bigcup_{i \in S} A(i) \right|.$$

The **Weighted Attribute Diversity**, $\mathcal{WA}$, of a set S equals the weighted average of the distinct attributes present in the population of types according to a vector of positive weights $\lambda = (\lambda_1, \lambda_2, \ldots, \lambda_A)$, where $\sum_{a=1}^{A} \lambda_a = 1$,

$$\mathcal{WA}(S) = \sum_{a \in \cup_i A(i)} \lambda_a.$$

Before discussing these two measures of diversity, I make a distinction between *measures* of diversity and *valuations* of diversity. Suppose that the weights on attributes, λ, originate from some objective criterion, such as the average distance from that attribute to all others. If so, then weighted attribute diversity can be interpreted as a measure. Alternatively, the weights might come from preferences. In considering the value of species, people might value warm, cuddly attributes more than sharp, fierce attributes. In this case, weighted attribute diversity should be interpreted as a *value* function, not a diversity measure.[22]

The relevance of attribute diversity measures hinges on the *transferability* of attributes and the *separability* of their functions. In economic contexts, attributes can be transferred from one type to another at low cost, as I cover later when comparing creative and evolutionary systems. Bluetooth technology can be transferred from a computer to a car to a tractor at low cost. The same cannot be said of the attribute "breathing through a hole in the top of your head." Dolphins can do it. Humans, try as they might, cannot adopt the attribute. Given that traits cannot be transferred in ecosystems, saving a trait has greater value in an ecosystem than it does in an economy. As a result, ecologists care more about preserving species than traits.

To see this more vividly, consider attributes as sets of skills possessed by people in an economy. Two of those skills might be the ability to start a fire using only flint and some straw; another might be to build a shelter. If stranded in a chilly forest, the group doesn't care who among them possesses those skills so long as someone in the collective does. In contrast, a person in need of an appendectomy prefers that the skill package (*good hand-eye coordination, sound judgment, medical knowledge*) resides in a single person rather than be spread among people. In the former case, the skills are separable. In the latter case, they are not. Adding up attributes makes more sense the more separable the attributes' functionalities.

Disjoint Population Measures

Each of the diversity measures I have discussed so far considers a single population. We might also want to measure the difference between two populations. Disjoint population measures apply to pairs of sets of types. The first measure, the *joint number of types*, equals the number of unique species if the two sets are combined. The second measure, the *number of non-overlapping types*, equals the number of types that belong to exactly one of the two sets. Whittaker (1972) refers to the first as *beta* diversity and the latter as *gamma* diversity. The measures I cover rely only on the number of types, but attributes-based measures could be constructed along similar lines.

Disjoint Population Diversity

Given two sets of types, S_1 and S_2, let the **Joint Number of Types** equal the total number of unique types in the two sets:

$$\mathcal{J}(S_1, S_2) = |S_1 \cup S_2|$$

Let the **Number of Non-overlapping Types** equal the total number of types that belong to a single one of the sets:

$$\mathcal{NV}(S_1, S_2) = |S_1 \cup S_2| - |S_1 \cap S_2|$$

These measures can be used to capture differences between ecosystems (or economies). If we hold the number of types in each set—for example, in an ecosystem or an economy—constant, an increase in the *joint number of types* corresponds to an increase in the *number of non-overlapping types.*

Capturing Diversity's Effects in Complex Systems

These formal measures of diversity prove useful in both empirical and theoretical investigations. Empirical tests that diversity has some effect require a characterization of diversity. The existence of multiple measures for diversity enables researchers to choose the measure that best captures the relevant diversity—does the effect depend on the number of types or on the distribution of types? Sometimes the choice of measure, in particular the widespread use of the *diversity index,* may owe as much to precedent as it does to logic.

In most cases, political and economic competition or ecosystem composition, the theory suggests that the distribution matters. For example, an election with three parties, one of which gets 98 percent of the vote, is not as competitive as one in which two parties split the vote nearly equally. Similarly, an ecosystem dominated by one species is not as diverse as one in which the species are balanced.

How diversity gets measured in practice depends on the question being asked. In a market, the government may care about the level of competition, and a sociologist may care more about the set of available choices. The measure used also depends on available data. Scientists may be able to identify the number of firms or the number of species, but getting measures of the distribution may be difficult. Moreover, which variable to use to measure proportions may not be obvious. The size of a firm can be captured by its sales, profits, or market share. The size of a species can be measured by biomass, energy usage, or number of the species in the population.

3

THE CREATION AND EVOLUTION OF DIVERSITY

Every species has come into existence coincident both in
space and time with a pre-existing closely allied species.
—A. R. WALLACE

The natural world supports incredible diversity: there are
more than thirty thousand species of ants and millions of
species of beetles. The British scientist J.B.S. Haldane reput-
edly once quipped, "the Creator, if he exists, has an inordinate
fondness for beetles." The world constructed by humans has
amazing diversity as well: we produce approximately one
million new books each year and probably at least that many
new recipes, including (I'm not making this up) Captain
Crunch Chicken. Diversity abounds, but it has limitations.
Only a few hundred species of hummingbirds exist, and
despite millions of computer programmers, only a handful of
computer operating systems. In the next two chapters I will
discuss the mechanisms that *produce* and *sustain* diversity, as
well as the forces that *constrain* it. I hope to come to a more
satisfying explanation of this diversity than the idiosyncratic
likes and dislikes of the divinity.

In this chapter, I focus on the production and maintenance of diversity. Where does it come from? How is it maintained? In the next chapter, I turn to constraints on its growth. Why do we see lots of diversity in some domains and less in others? In both chapters, I endeavor to find insights that are applicable across traditional disciplines. The effectiveness of this broad approach hinges partly on the existence of sufficient similarity between domains such that we can map concepts, insights, and theories from one to another. Of course, to say that an economy resembles an organism or that a legal system works like an immune system does not mean that the systems are identical. It just means that they share enough features that causal relationships we discover in one domain generally hold in the other.

I restrict my examples in these next two chapters to biological systems, economies, and systems of ideas, or what others have called "meme" systems (Dawkins 1976). This means omitting physical systems, legal systems, political systems, the Internet, and many more. This restriction is due to lack of space. The three systems I have chosen to cover differ in two important respects, which help us maximize what we learn from them. First, biological systems evolve, while economies and idea systems both evolve and are subject to creative changes by purposeful actors. Second, economies and biological systems are physical systems, while idea systems are informational or virtual. The nature and implications of these two important distinctions—between *evolutionary* and *creative* and between *physical* and *virtual*—will become clearer as I move along.

The distinction between creative and evolutionary systems is central to my analysis. Creative and evolutionary systems differ in important respects. The former have the potential for much more diversity, owing to the fact that new ideas need not be viable initially. They can still attract money from venture capitalists or publishing houses. In creative systems, the search for new ideas is not locally constrained. New types can emerge ex nihilo, out of whole cloth. On the other hand, creative systems may be constrained by cultural or scientific conventions, whereas evolutionary systems are not. Evolution will try just about anything—so long as it can get there.

This constant searching implies that in the absence of constraints and selection, evolutionary systems will tend to produce more and more diversity. McShea and Brandon (2010) refer to this phenomenon of increasing diversity as the *Zero-Force Evolutionary Law*. They show this increase in diversity occurs at all levels from molecules to cells to organ systems. This constant push toward greater diversity, they argue, creates complexity. Thus, their zero-force evolutionary law lies at the core of any explanation of biological complexity.

To say that diversity increases, we need to clarify which type of diversity. Recall from the previous chapter the distinctions between diversity within a type (variation), diversity across types, and diversity of community composition. In this chapter I focus mostly on diversity within and across types—the first two types of diversity. I describe five causes of variation. The first four—*mutation, inversion, recombination* (or copying), and *transfer*—come from evolutionary theory. The fifth, *representational diversity*, originated in the study of innovation but has recently been applied to genetics. I then describe how systems produce diversity across types. This has been studied extensively by ecologists, by scholars of innovation, and by cultural anthropologists. I describe six causes of diversity across types—*isolation, rugged landscapes, coupled landscapes, local interactions, temporal variation,* and *coordination.*

Importantly, all of the biological causes of diversity rely on variation within types in order to produce diversity across types. That's because evolution cannot take leaps. I don't mean to imply in any way that accumulated variations are not a force in the production of new types in creative systems as well. They are. The Hula Hoop can be seen as accumulated modifications in the bamboo hoops used by Australians,[23] and the modern automobile as the product of accumulated variations to the original horseless carriage (Arthur 2009).

The causes of community level diversity appear to be different in kind yet similar in spirit. When we take into account interactions between types, we begin to see the construction of local environments that support particular types. The creation of these local environments puts in motion a path-dependent series of events. As a result, communities come to differ. This logic plays out cleanly in the ecological context. To show how it transfers to the economic domain, I show how community diversity emerges in a model of chain stores that I wrote with Troy Tassier (2007). But first, I describe some basic mechanisms for producing variation.

Mechanisms for Producing Variation

In describing the mechanisms for producing variation, I start in the biological world but aim to connect the models to creative domains. I rely on a simple model in which genotype, phenotype, and function are equivalent. Thus, a change in a gene results in a change in attributes and function. This is a strong assumption and one that is factually incorrect. Making it simplifies an already dense presentation of the main concepts and allows me to skip over a lot of biological particulars.

One of the particulars that I will need later in my analysis of robustness concerns the relationship between phenotypic variation and genetic variation: differences in function versus differences in genes. We see much less of the former than the latter. If every genetic mutation produced a phenotypic change, then evolution would run amok. We'd be awash in diversity.[24] Krakauer and Plotkin (2002) describe three mechanisms that reduce the effects of genotypic variation on phenotypes: *canalization*: developmental suppression of differences, *neutrality*: phenotypic similarity, and *redundancy*: multiple encodings of the same phenotypic expression. In plain language, canalization means that development prevents the differences from getting expressed. Neutrality means that the genetic differences produce similar phenotypes. And redundancy means that the same outcome gets coded in multiple ways. Later, I'll distinguish a type of redundancy called degeneracy, but for the moment, I'm trying my best to present complex biology in plain English.

In this section, I consider four classic mechanisms: *mutation, inversion, recombination*, and *transfer*. I then show that analogs of each of these mechanisms operate in economic and idea systems. I conclude this section with a fifth mechanism, *representational diversity*. Representational diversity plays a more central role in creative systems, but it can occur in biological systems through redundant representations in a way I make formal.

Before I get too far, I need to lay down some stylized facts about the biological world that are relevant to understanding genetic evolution. At the finest grain that we know for certain, matter consists of quarks, muons, bosons, and things like that. Below that may be high-dimensional strings, or who knows what? Anyway, atoms combine to form molecules and molecules form *nucleotides*. These, not genes, are the fundamental units for evolution. Nucleotides have three parts: a nitrogen base (A,C,G,T), a sugar molecule, and a phosphate molecule. A *gene* is a sequence of nucleotides. These sequences have specific orders. Again, the details are superfluous, but suffice it to say that some orders play important functions and others appear not to. The value that a *gene* assumes among these many possibilities is called an *allele*.

Chromosomes, sequences of genes, are where much of the action takes place.[25] Humans have two copies of each chromosome and thus the full human genome is referred to as *diploid*.[26] Many people erroneously believe that sexual reproduction implies a diploid genome. Not true. Sexual species can be haploid, diploid, tetraploid, and even octoploid.

Sexual reproduction matters in many ways (see Low 2001). I won't be able to get into all of the ways that it matters here. My focus will be primarily on the benefits of recombination that sexual reproduction allows. Most important among these is the potential to take large jumps in genetic space yet maintain functionality.

Mutation

The first biological mechanism, *mutation*, is by far the simplest and easiest to explain. Let an *entity* be described by a sequence of 0s and 1s of length N. I refer to each of these as a *bit* so as to not offend the sensibilities of ecologists. Suppose I have an entity that can be represented by eight bits:

Original: 00010001

Suppose that the entity asexually reproduces. In copying itself, the species might make an error, the result being that the new entity would differ from the original on one or more of the bits. The mutated copy might look as follows:

Mutant: 00010000

Notice that the last bit takes value 0 and not value 1. In biological systems, by a mutation, I mean a change in DNA. This could be caused by radiation, viruses, or transcription errors. In an economic system, mutations can correspond to *errors*, such as when someone makes a mistake in a chemical recipe. They can also arise through *experimentation*. An idea or product, be it linear regression or the extension cord, does not remain fixed for all time. People alter it. Those alterations can be by accident or by intent. In either case, the change can be thought of as a mutation.

In biological systems, every reproduction involves some amount of mutation. This creates the potential for *genetic drift*. As I have mentioned genetic drift in passing twice already, nonbiologists might benefit from a formal definition. I begin by describing *drift* in a replicator setting. Imagine a school with 100 students. On a given day, each student either wears a hat or does not wear a hat. Suppose that each morning, each student's decision whether to wear a hat is a random choice, and that the probability that she chooses to wear a hat equals the proportion of people wearing hats the previous day. So, if 62 people wore hats the day before, each student chooses to wear a hat with probability 0.62.

If we let this process run, the number of hats worn each day will randomly drift. It may go from 62 to 64 to 61 and so on. The same can happen within species or in ecologies. If selection on an attribute is low, or if the attribute makes no contribution to fitness, then the number of that type will change, not unlike the number of hats. It'll be a random walk.[27]

If we take this same idea and apply it to diploid chromosomes, we get a more complicated model. If one parent has allele values AA and the other parent has allele values BB, then the child will be AB. But when an AB parent and an AB parent have a child, the result could be AB, BB, or AA. Over time, the population will drift across these three possibilities. Of course, if the population is large enough, then the law of large numbers kicks in and there should be no genetic drift. This can be stated formally as the Hardy-Weinberg principle (Edwards 1977). The principle states that in large populations lacking mutations, selection, disturbances, and local interactions the distribution of allele frequencies will attain equilibrium. Those conditions—no mutation, no local interaction, and large populations—are strong and won't hold in most systems. Hence, drift happens. And it is a major cause of diversity.

Though the topic of drift gets closest study in genetics, the phenomenon occurs in many other complex systems as well. Language, fashion, ideas all exhibit drift. In fact, any complex system in which selection does not operate strongly along some dimension is likely to experience drift. In social systems, that drift may be beneficial for reasons I discuss later in the context of March's (1991) model of exploration and exploitation.

Inversion

The second mechanism, *inversion*, occurs when a sequence of bits is reversed. In biological systems, this occurs when a chromosome or part of one gets copied in reverse order. The frequency of inversion depends on the species and the particular gene. Often they do not result in abnormalities. Inversion can be seen in the example below, instead of copying the subsequence of bits 110, inversion causes the bits to be copied as 011.

Original: 11000000

Inverted first three bits: 01100000

Inversion can be thought of as a big mistake, a much bigger mistake than mutation. It's also a mistake that takes a particular form, namely, reversing a segment of DNA. In creating new products or new ideas, copying does not take place by piecing together pieces of DNA. It involves putting together physical parts or ideas. Inversion does occur in economic systems and the world of ideas, and it can result in innovations—rather than making a grilled cheese sandwich with the cheese on the inside, a chef might grill the cheese on the outside (these are tasty, by the way). More often than not, inversions are probably not beneficial, such as the time in third grade when the boy in front of me wore his sweater backward.

Recombination

The third mechanism, *recombination*, occurs when portions of bits from each of two strings are combined to form a new string. In biological systems recombination occurs during sexual reproduction where offspring take some genes from one parent and some from the other. Crossover can be modeled as follows. Assume the following two parents:

Parent 1: 00<u>000000</u>   *Parent 2*: 11<u>1100</u>00

An offspring who takes the third through sixth bits from Parent 2 and the first and last two bits from the Parent 1 would look like this:

Offspring: 00110000

Though we think of recombination as a biological mechanism, something like it also exists in the economy (skate shoes) and in the world of ideas (airwave auctions). The classic examples of cross-fertilization of ideas describe the creation of a new type. Arthur (2009) gives many historical examples of how recombination has been a source of innovation. Here, I am focusing on variation within type. This covers fields as diverse as music and technology. When Bruce Springsteen claims Woody Guthrie and Bob Dylan as influences, he's not saying that his music merely combines ideas from Woody and Bob—there's some Chuck Berry in there as well—but at a metaphorical level he's describing a process of recombination of taking bits and pieces from other artists.

Notice that recombination differs from mutation and inversion in two important respects. First, it can only work with existing differences. Therefore, when applying recombination, *diversity begets diversity*: the more diverse the population of species, products, or ideas to be reproduced, the more diverse the offspring. Second, recombination moves in the direction of existing entities. Mutation can flip any bit to any value. Crossover only flips bit values to match some member of the population. Therefore, though a more intelligent way of producing variation, recombination is less innovative. Crossover can only include what's already in the population. It cannot create anything new.

Transfer

The fourth mechanism, *transfer*, occurs when a portion of one sequence of bits is transferred to another. This sequence of bits can be thought of as a favorable attribute. In the world of products, this can be something as simple as a cup holder. Transfer happens quickly and easily in the worlds of products and ideas. Once developed, the cup holder could be transferred from lawn chairs, to cars, to pontoon boats. A similar process occurs with ideas. Techniques like calculus, linear programming, and spectral analysis quickly spread among scholars.

Transfer does not happen for large species. A turtle cannot look at a tiger and horizontally transfer strong, quick legs. In microscopic biological entities like plasmids, extra DNA that resides in bacteria and eukaryotic organisms that is capable of replication, transfer does occur. Small bits of DNA get swapped like email messages. As a result, plasmids have incredible variation.[28]

The effect of transfer can be thought of as one-directional crossover. Rather than have an offspring, one entity just

copies part of another. In the example below, the transferee
copies the first four bits of the transferor.

Transferor: 10110000

Tranferee: 00001111

New Transferee: <u>1011</u>1111

   Transfer relies on existing bit values, and so, once again,
diversity begets diversity: The more variation in the population, the more that can be transfered. Though transfer
and crossover operate similarly, they differ in their speed.
Crossover requires sexual reproduction, and thus limits the
minimum time of differentiation to one generation, whereas
transfer can occur within a generation. In the world of
products and ideas, we see more transfer than crossover.
When a product adds some attribute of another product—
such as a technological capability—it engages in transfer.

Representational Diversity

The final mechanism for producing variation, *representational
diversity*, works in conjunction with the other mechanisms.
I describe how representational diversity produces variation
in two ways. I first show how it operates in the context of
products or ideas. I then show how biology may pull off the
same trick even though species have a single representation
DNA.
   Suppose that there exist four products (respectively, ideas)
denoted by *A*, *B*, *C*, and *D*. Suppose also that we have two

ways of representing these products using binary strings of length two: *Representation 1 (R1)* and *Representation 2 (R2)*:

Diverse Representations

Product	R1	R2
A	00	00
B	01	01
C	10	11
D	11	10

Imagine an employee tasked with making product A, who experiments or makes a mistake that causes A to *mutate*. In representation R1, the one-bit mutations (01 and 10) correspond to B and C. In representation R2, the one-bit mutations (again 01 and 10) correspond to B and D. Having two different representations of the products B, C, and D enlarges the set of products that can be reached by one-bit mutations. As a result, representational diversity plus mutation leads to more variation than would occur through mutation alone. Similar arguments hold for the interactions between representational diversity and crossover, inversion, and transfer.

This is an important idea, so I want to drive it home with an example. Consider a company that dyes T-shirts green. The company operates two production lines, each with two colors of dye. The first line, which corresponds to R1, has the colors green and yellow. To make a green shirt, a worker turns the knob to add green dye but does not turn the knob to add yellow dye. This can be encoded as $G = 1$, $Y = 0$. Suppose that worker makes a mistake. A single mistake could lead to either a white shirt ($G = 0$, $Y = 0$) or a chartreuse shirt ($G = 1$, $Y = 1$). On the second line, the two colors are yellow and blue, and both knobs must be turned ($B = 1$, $Y = 1$) to make a green shirt. If a worker on this line errs, he makes either a blue shirt ($B = 1$, $Y = 0$) or a yellow ($B = 0$, $Y = 1$) shirt. Thus, different representations of the same product create different likely mutations. Once again, diversity begets diversity.

Biological evolution, given its reliance on DNA, would seem to be precluded from exploiting diverse representations. A deeper look at the map from genotype to phenotype shows that this may not be true. Evolution can exploit diverse representations through *neutral mutations* (Wagner 2005).[29] Neutral mutation occurs when a change in genotype results in no change in phenotype. This can be seen through an example. Suppose that there exist four phenotypes, denoted by A, B, C, and D. Representations R1 and R2 encode these phenotypes as binary strings of length two. In *Representation 3 (R3)* the four phenotypes are encoded using binary strings of length three. Here, though, each phenotype can (and does) appear twice. I will refer to this as a *redundant representation*.

A Redundant Representation

Phenotype	R3	Phenotype	R3
A	000	A	100
B	001	B	101
C	010	C	111
D	011	D	110

Let's start with a homogeneous population. Suppose that every member of the population has phenotype A and genotype 000. The one-bit mutations of A are $B = 001$, $C = 010$ and $A = 100$. These mutant phenotypes B and C may or may not survive. The third mutant, though, phenotype A with genotype 100, definitely survives, as it has the same phenotype as the rest of the population. Such mutations are called *neutral*. Over time, then, we might expect the population of As to contain both genotypes 000 and 100. We might even think of the first bit as "junk DNA," as it has no effect on phenotype. Notice, though, that the neutral mutant (genotype 100) provides a diverse representation of A. The one-bit mutations from genotype 100 are $B = 101$, $D = 110$, and $A = 000$.

Here's the key insight: phenotype D can now be reached, whereas it could not before. Thus, by creating redundant representations that include neutral mutations, evolution produced, in effect, diverse representations. And, as shown above, two ways of representing the same phenotype can result in more one bit mutants. I take up this concept of redundant representations with greater specificity when I discuss degeneracy as a source of robustness.

Mechanisms for Creating and Evolving Diverse Types

Mutation, drift, crossover, inversion, transfer, and representational diversity produce variation (differences within a type). I now turn to how a diversity of types emerges. In population biology, this is known as speciation. As discussed in the previous chapter, the distinction between variation within and across species isn't as clean as might be thought. It's clear that alligators differ from bluebirds, but dividing up all those orchids and warblers gets messy.

My discussion of the evolution and creation of type diversity relies on the *rugged landscape model* and its offspring, the *dancing landscapes model*. A rugged landscape is a graphical representation of a function defined over several variables in which the elevation of any type corresponds to its *payoff* or *value.* In biology, this *payoff* equals fitness, in economics, it equals profits or market share, and in the world of ideas, it could correspond to some combination of relevance and resonance. Thus, the payoff to a beetle may equal the number of viable offspring it produces. The payoff to a magazine salesperson may be the number of subscriptions she sells, and the payoff to an academic may be the number of conference invitations she receives.

The rugged landscape model assumes that fitness does not change. That would be true if fitness did not depend on features of other species. In reality, the value of size to one species usually depends on the size of other species in its ecosystem. This interdependence means that the fitness landscape for a species will fluctuate due to adaptations by other species. I will refer to these coupled rugged landscapes as *dancing landscapes.* Dancing landscapes capture co-evolutionary processes.

For now, what's important is that selection operates on both rugged and dancing landscapes. By that I mean that types that are not of sufficient elevation will not survive. Species that don't produce enough viable offspring, firms that don't make normal economic profits, and ideas that don't attract many followers die out. In order to understand what causes diversity, we first need to understand what survives selection.

In what follows, I describe six causes of diversity across types that build from this idea of landscapes: *isolation (different landscapes)*, *different peaks* on the same landscape, *coupled landscapes* which create diverse attractors, *local interactions*, *coordination*, and *temporal variation*. These six causes are similar to what one would find in an introductory textbook in biology (I'll show that). These causes explain the diversity of products and ideas that exist in the world as well as the diversity of species in ecosystems. These are meant not to be exhaustive, but to capture the main causes.

Evolutionary theory distinguishes four modes of speciation: *geographic heterogeneity* (allopatry), *isolation of a small subpopulation* (peripatry), *divergent neighboring niches* (perapatry), and *diverse niches in a common environment* (sympatry). Before proceeding farther, I will make a crude distinction between a subspecies and a species. The difference is subtle. Consider a species that separates into two populations in disparate locations. If those two populations diverge, we might consider one a subspecies of the other. If the two species reunite, they may interbreed. They may not. If they do, their brief time apart would be considered just some youthful experimentation. If they do not interbreed, then they've become sympatric species, each carving out a distinct niche.

When I discuss speciation, I'm often talking about subspeciation—the creation of a subpopulation that differs. I gloss over whether that subspecies can interbreed with the original species. I'm accept this blurring of categories because I'm also covering ideas and products. They don't breed with one another, so they have no clear analog to species or subspecies.

Selection

In ecological, economic, and ideological contexts, selection drives diversity. This might seem paradoxical. After all, selection drives out the unfit. It reduces variation and should work against the creation of diverse types. Without selection, mutation, recombination, and the like would lead to runaway variation. Nevertheless, differences in the environment (either extant or created) can also enable selection to produce type diversity.

Replicator Dynamics: Before I can describe how selection produces diversity, I must first show how selection reduces diversity. I'll do this using *replicator dynamics*. The *replicator equation* provides a convenient way to represent selection among a population of diverse types. For convenience, assume that time can be divided into discrete periods and that selection occurs between periods. The replicator equation gives the proportion of each type in the population in the next period as a function of the type's payoff and its current proportion. Types that earn above average payoffs increase in proportion, while types that earn below average payoffs decrease in proportion. The amount of increase or decrease depends on a type's proportion in the current population and on its relative payoff.

The Replicator Equation

Let $(\pi_1, \pi_2, \ldots, \pi_N)$ denote the payoffs of N distinct types, and let $(p_1^t, p_2^t, \ldots, p_N^t)$ denote the types' proportions in the population at time t. Let $\bar{\pi}^t$ equal the mean payoff at time t:

$$\bar{\pi}^t = \sum_{i=1}^{N} p_i^t \pi_i.$$

The **replicator equation** defines p_i^{t+1} as follows:

$$p_i^{t+1} = p_i^t \frac{\pi_i}{\bar{\pi}^t}.$$

For the moment, assume that payoffs remain fixed over time, that no two types earn the same payoff, and that the initial population contains every type in strictly positive proportions. Given these three assumptions, replicator dynamics wipe out all but the type with the highest payoff. Hence, the well-worn phrase: survival of the fittest. The rate at which this occurs is geometric. That is, starting from equal proportions of types, after T periods, the proportion of each type is proportional to its fitness raised to the Tth power. We see this in the Repeated Replicator Equation below.

The Repeated Replicator Equation

Let $(\pi_1, \pi_2, \ldots, \pi_N)$ denote the payoffs of N distinct types. Assume that, initially, each type comprises $\frac{1}{N}$th of the population. After T applications of the replicator dynamic, the proportion of type i equals

$$p_i^T = \frac{\pi_i^T}{\sum_{j=1}^N \pi_j^T}.$$

Even though selection geometrically favors the more fit, it along with mutation is one of the main drivers of diversity. The question of how much of diversity is due to selection and how much is due to mutation is open to debate. The *neutral theory* of evolution (Kimura 1983) ascribes most of the weight to mutation and genetic drift, which I described previously. The debate hinges on whether most mutations are neutral, that is, have no strong effect on selection, or whether there exist enough mutations that confer sufficient selective advantage to prevent genetic drift.

Selection as Swarming a Peak

My analysis of selection borrows from ecology and from computer science. What I describe is a variant of biological mechanisms and a *genetic algorithm* (Holland 1975). A genetic algorithm begins with a population of entities. Each member of the population can be represented by a sequence of 0s and 1s. Think of this like DNA. For convenience, I assume a *fitness function* that assigns each of those strings a *fitness*. The fitness function maps the binary strings into the real numbers.[30]

These assumptions create a *landscape*, where each entity is a point on a map and the entity's fitness is represented as an elevation. Landscapes are often categorized by the number of peaks they have. A single-peaked landscape such as the one shown in Figure 3.1 (also called a Mt. Fuji landscape) poses little challenge to a selection operator. By that I mean, almost any rule for selecting better members of the population will locate the single peak on the landscape. Many landscapes are *rugged*, that is, they have lots of peaks. In a few pages, I'll show how rugged landscapes produce diverse types.

Figure 3.1. A Mt. Fuji landscape.

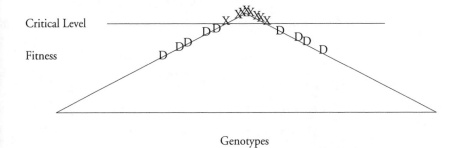

Genotypes

Figure 3.2. A critical level on a Mt. Fuji landscape.

Given a diverse population, selection drives out the unfit, or, alternatively, allows the fit to survive. Here, by *fitness*, I mean the standard biological representation of it—the ability to reproduce. For a species, we know what reproduction means. For an idea or product or restaurant to be reproduced it must be interesting or profitable enough to get copied, either by its inventor or by someone else. Goods and ideas must survive in the marketplace.

To capture survivability, I can emend the figure in Figure 3.2 and include a *critical level* of fitness—in effect, a water line. Any member of the species with fitness below the water line drowns (denoted by *D*). Any member with fitness above the water line survives and has the potential to reproduce.

One final point on selection relates to those attributes not subject to selection. They'll be diverse. With no selection to stop genetic and ecological drift, differences can run wild. For example, some evidence shows that songbirds bred in captivity display greater variation in the songs they sing. This diversity arises because no selection takes place on the songs of these birds. Selection primarily operates on beauty

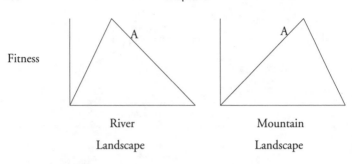

Fitness

River   Mountain

Landscape   Landscape

Figure 3.3. Distinct peaks on related landscapes.

(Lanier 2010). We can take this logic and construct some fun thought experiments. If all species lost the ability to see color, then color would no longer be subject to selective pressures. If after several thousand years, we could suddenly see color, we'd probably encounter a crazy multicolored reality.

Now that we have a basic understanding of selection and landscapes, we can explore how selection acts on populations to produce diversity.

Isolation (Different Landscapes)

The first explanation for how selection can produce type diversity relies on different landscapes. The version that I present here builds from the work of Ernst Mayr (2001). Suppose that we take two identical populations of dogs and place them in two distinct ecologies. The first population might live in a river valley, and the second might live on a mountaintop. This separation could arise through a geologic event such as an earthquake or volcanic eruption, or it could be human created. Figure 3.3 shows the average member of the population A and its fitness on each of the two landscapes.

In the river landscape, the population will drift to the left due to selection on fitness until it reaches the peak. In the mountain landscape, the population will drift to the right. If the peaks in the two landscapes differ sufficiently, the result will be two species.

In the stark version that I have just presented, the two landscapes are not connected. In reality, the river landscape might gradually transition to the mountain landscape. In this transition area between the river and the mountain, we might find a gradient of genotypic and phenotypic differences. Biologists refer to these populations of species as a *cline*. Clines make the identification of species and subspecies difficult.

The landscape analogy also applies to products and behaviors. Take the case of shoes. Here, instead of fitness, altitude would represent *functionality* or *profit*. In the river landscape, people might wear moccasins, while in the mountain landscape people might prefer hiking boots. For both dogs and footwear, selection in heterogeneous contexts produces type diversity.

Different Peaks

The second explanation for how selection creates type diversity relies on the existence of multiple peaks on the same rugged fitness landscape. This cause forms part of Sewall Wright's *shifting balance theory* (1982). Shifting balance theory assumes that the population divides into small subpopulations that can undergo genetic drift. This allows them to leap or crawl across valleys on the rugged landscape to find new peaks. If the new peak is higher than the old peak, then the population can shift toward the subpopulation on the new peak (see Figure 3.4). Hence, the balance shifts.

For illustrative purposes, I focus on how a particular attribute, the weight of a laptop's metal casing, may create multiple peaks. If the casing is too light, the laptop lacks structural integrity. Once structural integrity has been reached, additional weight has no increase in integrity, so functionality falls. This creates the first peak. At some point, adding more weight insulates the laptop from damage when dropped from, say, an unzipped backpack. So weight starts to increase functionality. However, after some point, adding more weight adds no further insulation and makes the laptop too heavy to carry; thus creating a second peak. Functionality as a function of weight, therefore, looks as follows:

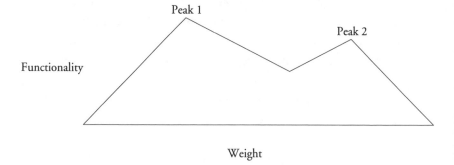

Figure 3.4. A landscape with multiple peaks.

In the case of laptops, selection normally occurs in the testing laboratory or the marketplace. In the figure above, the two peaks have different heights. Under severe selection pressures, only the strongest (those at Peak 1) would survive. But that result assumes that the lightweight laptops compete against the heavyweights—that the two products meet the same market. It could be that the people who buy heavy-weight laptops would never purchase a lightweight laptop. If so, laptops at both peaks may survive.

Wright's shifting balance theory produces another interesting insight. If a landscape has multiple peaks, and if the initial population is small, it could get sucked into one peak without ever exploring the others. Suppose that a small group of finches separates from the larger population and that these finches have genotypes that place them near Peak 2. The result will be that ensuing populations resemble their founders.[31] This can be thought of as a form of premature convergence.

Coupled Landscapes

The third way in which selection can produce type diversity is through *coupled landscapes*. Coupled landscapes capture interdependencies in payoffs. The success of a species depends on the success of its predators and on what it consumes. As Levin (2000) points out, success has its costs. A species must avoid being so successful that it wipes out its food source: The fitness of a bird depends on the abundance of worms.

Biologists refer to coupled landscape models as *co-evolutionary*. Co-evolution differs from what economists call *competition* in a subtle way. Competition takes the attributes of the actors as fixed. In models of product competition, attributes like price and quality determine market share. So, for example, the profitability of an airline depends on its routes, pricing, and fleet, and on similar features of its competitors. The analysis of profitability in introductory economics is static. Each firm gets a share of the market.

In a co-evolutionary model, the species attributes evolve over time. In co-evolution, a species' fitness landscape depends on the actions, attributes, and population sizes of other species. This means that the landscapes of the interdependent species perform a coupled dance. Movements on one landscape shift the heights on other landscapes. When the gazelle become faster, the fitness of extra bulk on a lion falls. When one species adapts a poison to fight off a predator, what ecologists call alleopathy, it dramatically alters the landscape for the other species.

To show how coupled landscapes produce diversity, I construct an extremely simple evolutionary model based on a coordination game. The players in this game are squirrels and oaks. I focus on a single attribute of each player: size. I assume that squirrels take one of two sizes, small or large (s or l) and that so do trees (S or L). In reality, of course, the number of possible sizes would be much larger, but two proves sufficient for generating the intuition.

The payoffs to squirrels and trees are given in the matrix below. The matrix reveals *interdependent payoffs*. The payoff to a small squirrel living on a small oak tree equals eight, but the payoff to the same squirrel on a large oak equals only four.

		Squirrels	
		s	*l*
Oaks	*S*	8,8	4,4
	L	4,4	12,12

Imagine two islands, each populated with oaks and squirrels. On the first island, half of the squirrels are large and half are small, similarly, half of the oaks are large and half are small. Half of the small squirrels will live near small oaks. Their fitness will equal eight. Half will live near large oaks, and their fitness will equal four. Therefore, the average fitness of the small squirrels will equal six. A similar calculation shows that the average fitness of large squirrels will equal eight. Selection will favor large squirrels, so in the next generation more than half of the squirrels should be large. Identical logic shows that large oaks will be more fit and therefore will grow in the population. This process will continue until only large squirrels and large oaks populate the first island.[32]

On the second island, suppose that only one-fourth of the squirrels and oaks are large. On this island, the average fitness of a small squirrel equals seven ($7 = \frac{3}{4} \times 8 + \frac{1}{4} \times 4$) and the average fitness of large squirrels equals six. On this island, selection favors small squirrels and small oaks. Over time, both will come to dominate the island.

This example considers only variation in size, but if that variation is severe enough, or if variation arises on other attributes, then distinct species may emerge. It may become impossible for the squirrels on one island to reproduce with the squirrels on another island. Over time, the landscapes on two islands can become so different that one produces kangaroos and the other produces miniature horses.

The Limits to Dancing: Proficiency and Context: We've just seen how interdependent payoffs produce dancing landscapes using a model with only two actions. More realistic models of species adaptation (or market or political competition) would include multidimensional action spaces. Some choices of actions unilaterally improve fitness, profits, or market share. I will refer to these as *proficient* adaptations. When a species improves its energy efficiency, its fitness improves independent of the context. Or, when a firm finds a way to lower its cost without sacrificing quality, it improves its profits independently of what its competitors do.

Most adaptations do not improve payoffs in all environments. When a firm increases its quality *and* its price, it might earn higher profits, but it also might not. The value of such an adaptation depends on the reactions of competitors. So, too, for a species that adapts. Whether or not the adaptation proves beneficial depends on the adaptations of other species. I will refer to these as *contextual* adaptations.[33]

The distinction between proficient adaptations and contextual adaptations proves useful in defining natural selection and evolution. Natural selection is the process through which traits that produce a reproductive advantage grow in the population. Thus, proficient adaptations, on average, increase in the population. Evolution, though, is more than just natural selection. It also includes ecological changes that result from selection.[34] Fitness, in an ecology (or a market), depends on the actions of others. In other words, many adaptations are contextual—they produce benefits in some instances but not in others. Kauffman (1993) created a model of coupled fitness landscapes that includes both types of adaptations. Some attributes have payoffs that depend on the attributes of other species and some attributes have payoffs that are independent of the attributes of others. Some parts of the landscapes dance. Some parts don't.

Local Interactions

In the coupled landscape model previously described, squirrels and oaks tend to be both large or both small. These are the only two stable equilibria. A single system supports small oaks or large oaks. Diversity exists across locations but not within a location. This homogeneity follows from the assumption of *random mixing*. In a random mixing model, each entity randomly interacts with all other entities. In many complex systems, entities interact locally. They're situated in geographic space. This is true of people and of naked mole rats. Limiting the interactions between entities, or agents, to be local increases diversity.

To show how local interactions allow more diversity to persist, I introduce a game known as the *pure coordination game*. In the pure coordination game, each agent, or player, must choose whether to shake or bow. If she meets another player who takes the same action, she gets a payoff of one. If she meets a player who takes the alternative action, she gets a payoff of zero.

Player 2

		Shake(S)	*Bow(B)*
Player 1	*Shake(S)*	**1,1**	**0,0**
	Bow(B)	**0,0**	**1,1**

First, consider random mixing in which each person plays a random collection of others. Suppose that there are an odd number of players. Each player randomly meets others and earns payoffs from those interactions. If I add a selection operator (note that here replication captures learning, not the death of the unfit), then over time, whichever action had been more common initially takes over the population. If the initial population contains 55 percent bowers, then eventually all players will bow.

Next, place these players on a grid and assume that a player (denoted by X) interacts with the four neighbors to its North (N), South (S), East (E), and West (W) as shown in the figure below. This creates *local interactions*.

	N	
W	X	E
	S	

Under local interactions, it's possible to support diversity. Consider the following configuration of shakers (S) and bowers (B). As in the Nowak and May model presented in Chapter 2, players are positioned on a checkerboard and each has four neighbors. We can then create a torus by connecting players on the top and bottom and on the right and left.

S	S	B	B	S	S	S
S	S	B	B	S	S	S
S	S	B	B	S	S	S
S	S	B	B	S	S	S
S	S	B	B	S	S	S
S	S	B	B	S	S	S
S	S	B	B	S	S	S

In this configuration, each bower has three neighbors who bow and one who shakes. Each shaker has at least three neighbors who shake. Therefore, each player optimizes by sticking with its current action, and diversity persists. If the players were to interact with everyone, then the shakers would take over the population. Though stylized, this example highlights a key point: *complex systems that include local interactions may be more likely to support diversity.*

Now, let's suppose we introduce a slight probability of error—sometimes a person bows when he should have shaken. In the random mixing model, once the population has converged on all shakers or bowers, the effect of the occasional error will be minimal. In the local interactions case, the effect will be quite different. If a handful of neighbors make the same error, that error can propagate through the network. Over the long haul, errors plus local interactions can result in a system that continually bounces back and forth between bowing and shaking (Ellison 1993).

Coordination

As I mentioned, the shake or bow game is an example of a *coordination* game. Coordination can also create type diversity in disjoint populations. If the members of two distinct populations coordinate, they reduce variation within their populations, but if they coordinate on different attributes, they produce distinct types. This counterintuitive insight forms the basis for complex systems models of cultural formation (Axelrod 1997; Bednar and Page 2007). For example, one population could become shakers and another could become bowers. These distinct, persistent behavioral differences between groups of people are a hallmark of culture.

Consider the following stylized model of cultural formation. Imagine two communities. Each community faces a collection of left (L) or right (R) games. They must decide to drive on the left or right, shake hands with the right or left hand, put forks on the right or left side of the plate, read from left to right or from right to left, etc. Assume that, initially, each individual randomly chooses an action in each game. I can then represent an individual as a string of Ls and Rs.

Person 1: LLRRLRLLRRRLR

Person 2: RLLRRRLLLRRLL

Initially, the two communities will exhibit substantial variation in behavior. Over time, people within each community
will have incentives to coordinate and variation will disappear.
If we look at a single community, we will see that all the
members choose identical behaviors. They'll drive on the left,
shake with the right, and put the fork on the left side of
the plate. There will be no variation. If we look at the other
community, we'll see that its members also all do the same
thing, but they do a *different* same thing. They may drive on
the right and put their forks on the right. This community's
"culture" differs from that of the other community.[35] The
two communities, therefore, contain different types of people.
Coordination causes that diversity.

Temporal Disturbances (Plus)

The final cause of diversity that I consider is temporal disturbances. Suppose that the environment changes—sometimes
it's hot and sometimes it's cold. These fluctuations would
seem to support a diversity of types: some that do well in
the heat and some that thrive in the cold. In ecology, this
intuition forms half of the *intermediate disturbance hypothesis*
(Grime 1973; Connell 1978; Johst and Huth 2005). The
interim disturbance hypothesis states that diversity rises and
then falls with the rate of temporal fluctuations. Noss (1996)
states that "one notable generalization of modern ecology is
that moderate levels of disturbance maximize the diversity of
habitats and species."

The logic that explains this stylized fact goes as follows: In stable environments, diversity should be low as selection leads to competitive exclusion. In less stable or noisier environments, diversity increases. Different species or variants of the same species should be more fit (obtain higher payoffs) depending on the state. If the states of nature change too frequently, then diversity should again be low, as only those species that do well on average should survive.

The interim disturbance hypothesis is distinct from the concept of *ecological succession* (Levin 2000). Oaks and hickories need established grasses for their seeds to germinate and grow. In a stable environment, grasses will lead to oaks. With no disturbances, a patch of forest would become all large trees. If fires occur with regularity, the patch will remain a grassland. Hence, Bob Grese, who manages the University of Michigan Nichols Arboretum, directs volunteers to burn the prairie near my home every year to prevent the succession to oaks.[36]

Here, I'm describing something different from succession. I'm imagining a single patch. That patch has some rate of disturbances. In order to grow, species B does not first need species A to be established. Instead, each species has a fitness that depends on the state of the environment. Different species do better in different states. I want to test the claim that interim levels of disturbance, that is, periodic changes in the state, preserve diversity. As compelling as this logic may sound, I find that it needs more assumptions. In a fluctuating environment, selective pressure alone proves insufficient to maintain diversity. Note: I am *not* questioning the empirical validity of the intermediate disturbance hypotheses. I am saying that diversity does not increase and then decrease as a function of the amount of noise in a standard model using only the replicator dynamic.

I devote time to this simple model for three reasons: First, the results highlight the importance of constructing models to work through logic. The stylized model of replicator dynamics and temporal disturbances won't produce the anticipated result. The failure to produce the expected result encourages us to think more deeply and to add more detail. Second, the model shows why sometimes combinations of assumptions matter. Temporal disturbances don't matter independently, but they do matter when we include spatial interactions. Third, the model provides a nice example of complex systems fanning out. In the model the types are beans, alfalfa, and carrots, but they could equally well be bearish investors, bullish investors, and balanced investors in a market. Balanced investing may be the best thing to do in the long run but a sequence of good states could result in the growth of bullish traders. Too many bulls can produce large events. Some analyses of stock market bubbles and collapses point to a lack of fluctuations (a long run up in prices) as driving diversity down and setting the stage for collapse.

The proof builds from an example. Suppose that there exist two equally likely possible states: dry (D) and wet (W). Suppose further that in each period, one of these two states arises randomly. Finally, suppose that the ecology consists of three kinds of plants: alfalfa (A), beans (B), and carrots (C). For the purposes of the example, assume alfalfa performs well in any weather, beans perform best if it rains, and carrots do best in dry weather. Let $\pi(X|S)$ denote the fitness of type X in state S.

π (Alfalfa | Dry) = 4 π (Alfalfa | Wet) = 4,

π (Beans | Dry) = 3 π (Beans | Wet) = 5,

π (Carrots | Dry) = 5 π (Carrots | Wet) = 3.

Suppose that states arrive in the sequence $WWDDW$ $DDDDWWW$. Intuition suggests that all three types would survive in reasonable proportions. Initially, beans would do best (WW), then carrots (DD). Alfalfa would survive because it does okay in both states. In the fifth period, beans would have a brief resurgence, but then the four Ds in a row would cause carrots to dominate. Finally, the three periods of W would enable the beans to reestablish themselves.

To show what happens in this model, I derive a two period replicator equation that takes into account the state of the world—that is, whether it is dry or wet. In the box below, I characterize this *two period, two state replicator equation*. This equation shows that the proportion of a population of any type after one period of state W, and one period of state D, depends on the type's initial proportion and on the product of its payoffs across the two states.

The product of two numbers does not depend on their order (five times four equals four times five). Therefore, the order in which states arise does not affect the population proportions. It follows that the proportions of the various types after the sequence of states WD must be the same as after the sequence of states DW. Moreover, given a longer sequence of states, switching any two adjacent states can have no effect on final proportions. This means that the population proportions after the sequence of states $WWDD$ would be

---

The Two Period, Two State Replicator Equation

Let $(\pi_1^S, \pi_2^S, \ldots, \pi_N^S)$ denote the payoffs of N distinct types in state $S \in \{W, D\}$. Let $(p_1^t, p_2^t, \ldots, p_N^t)$ denote these types proportions in the population at time t.

The **two period, two state replicator equation** defines $p_i^{t+2}(WD)$ after one period of W followed by one period of D as

$$p_i^{t+2}(WD) = p_i^t \frac{\pi_i^W \pi_i^D}{\sum_{j=1}^N \pi_j^W \pi_j^D p_j^t}.$$

N.B. The order in which the states arises does not matter: $p_i^{t+2}(WD) = p_i^{t+2}(DW)$.

---

the same as after the sequence $WDWD$, and it would also be the same as after the sequence $DDWW$. Each has two wet periods and two dry periods.

Here, I'm considering twelve periods, but the same logic holds. The fitness at the end of the twelve periods depends only on the product of the fitnesses in each period. As I am assuming wet and dry periods each occur six times, I need only calculate the fitness for each species for two periods, one wet and one dry. For the three species in the example, those products can be computed as follows:

$\pi(\text{Alfalfa} \mid \text{Dry}) \times \pi(\text{Alfalfa} \mid \text{Wet}) = 16,$
$\pi(\text{Beans} \mid \text{Dry}) \times \pi(\text{Beans} \mid \text{Wet}) = 15,$
$\pi(\text{Carrots} \mid \text{Dry}) \times \pi(\text{Carrots} \mid \text{Wet}) = 15.$

These simple calculations reveal alfalfa's advantage. If the population started out with equal proportions of beans, carrots, and alfalfa, then after one sequence of the states WD, 16/46 of the population would be alfalfa, 15/46 would be beans, and 15/46 would be carrots. Using the **repeated replicator equation**, after T sequences the proportion of alfalfa would equal:

$$\frac{16^T}{16^T + 15^T + 15^T}.$$

As T grows large, this converges to one, so in the not-so-long run, if wet and dry states continue to be equally likely, alfalfa will take over. For this simple model, the appropriate logic is not that of the intermediate disturbance hypothesis, but the logic of averaging—the type that does best on (geometric) average takes over.

Several caveats are in order. First, the fact that final diversity does not depend on the order does not mean that diversity along the way doesn't depend on fluctuations. To see this, toss out the alfalfa, so that we only have beans and carrots. The sequence of states $WDWDWDWDWDWD$ will maintain moderate levels of both beans and carrots. The sequence $WWWWWWDDDDDD$ will result in several periods in the middle in which most of the plants are beans. Only after a number of dry periods can the carrots catch up. In any given period (except the last), the first sequence of states produces the more even distribution across the two types.

Second, my simple replicator model did not include physical space, interactions between types, or population-dependent fitness. In real ecologies, the more of a species that exists, the less well it performs. This diminishing returns to type occurs because of a lack of food: too many robins create a shortage of worms. In other contexts, payoff-dependent fitness can point in the other direction. Recall from the coordination model that the more shakers that exist, the higher the payoff for being a shaker.

It's not difficult to construct models that include these extensions. Each could resurrect the interim disturbance hypothesis. Let's try adding physical space. Imagine that I plant the alfalfa, beans, and carrots in a long row as follows:

$$BBABCBCACCBC$$

For accounting purposes, assign a number from one to twelve to each site in the row and compute fitness as before. However, in this model, I assume a location can only be filled by one of the types at a neighboring location. For example, the type at location four in the next period can only be one of the types at locations three, four, and five this period. To simplify the analysis, I assume that we have long patches of each type and a large number of locations. I can then calculate the probability that a location with a bean becomes a carrot and so on. Consider the last bean plant in a patch that abuts an alfalfa plant (denoted in **bold**).

$$BBBBBB\mathbf{B}AAAAA$$

First, assume that the weather is dry. The fitness of the bean equals three and the fitness of the alfalfa equals four. Two of the three locations that could seed this location are beans and one is alfalfa; therefore, the probability that a bean grows there next period equals $\frac{6}{10}$. So, even though alfalfa is more fit, it is most likely the bean remains a bean. Furthermore, all beans in the interior of a patch remain beans. The net result is that selection moves along at a much slower pace. A similar calculation shows that the probability that the alfalfa plant remains an alfalfa plant equals $\frac{8}{11}$. These rules produce a random walk on the boundary, where the probability that an additional alfalfa plant grows equals $\frac{8}{11}$ times $\frac{4}{10}$ and the probability that an additional bean plant grows equals $\frac{3}{11}$ times $\frac{6}{10}$. In other words, about 30 percent of the time the boundary will move to the left (more alfalfa) and about 16 percent it will move to the right (more beans).[37]

With N locations and three types, there exist 3^N possible configurations. Given these rules, it is possible to derive the probability of moving from any one configuration to any other in a given period. This is called a *transition probability*.[38] Note that almost all of those transition probabilities will be zero. It's not possible for a location with a bean surrounded by beans to get a carrot plant in the next period. The transition probabilities depend on the state. If the weather is wet, beans will grow at the expense of carrots and alfalfa but alfalfa will outperform carrots, so alfalfa will eat into the boundary of carrot patches.

Suppose that periods alternate: wet then dry. The probability that beans increase on an alfalfa-bean boundary equals $\frac{18}{110}$, and the probability that the alfalfa increases equals $\frac{32}{110}$. In wet periods, the corresponding probabilities equal $\frac{50}{182}$ and $\frac{32}{182}$. After two periods, one wet and one dry, we have the following probabilities of changes in the number of beans and alfalfa plants at a bean-alfalfa boundary:

Outcome	Probability
Beans + 2	4.5%
Beans + 1	24.0%
No Change	40.8%
Alfalfa + 1	25.6%
Alfalfa + 2	5.1%

The table reveals a very slight drift toward alfalfa. Thus, adding geographic space to a model of fluctuations leads to a substantial decrease in the rate at which diversity decreases and resurrects the intermediate disturbance hypothesis. Now, disturbances can keep multiple types alive.

In this model, the types (plants) remain fixed. Animals and insects are not fixed. They can roam. Some animals and insects, particularly those that fly, can cover large distances. The more freedom the types have to move, the more likely they can fill open spots in the geography. The two models I discussed here represent the extremes. In the model without space, I am in effect assuming that any type can move anywhere. The result: survival of only the fittest. When species are fixed in place, then the less fit can survive for a long time. Thus, the ability to move should correlate with a reduction in diversity.

Diversity across Systems

In the previous two sections I discussed the mechanisms that cause variation and diversity across types. I now turn to the creation of diversity across systems. To show how systems differ, I rely on the concept of *path dependence* (Arthur 1994; Page 2006). I am going to construct a simplified version of a multi-city model of firm competition based on Page and Tassier (2007). That paper considered firms. Here I will consider competing Mexican fast food restaurants.

In the model, each restaurant chooses a type of food to serve. I'll assume that Mexican fast food has two attributes, *size* and *heat*, and that both size and heat can be assigned numbers from the set $\{1, 2, \ldots, 10\}$. For example, a burrito with size equal to two and heat equal to nine would be small and hot. Given this setup, a restaurant can be mapped into two-dimensional space where the horizontal dimension represents size and the vertical dimension represents heat. Following convention, I refer to this as the restaurant's *hedonic location*.

I now add a population of consumers. Each consumer has a *hedonic ideal point* that denotes that person's preferred attributes for Mexican fast food. Ideal points can also be mapped into a two-dimensional space. To avoid complicating the model, I assume that all burritos have the same price. Therefore, consumers will purchase from the restaurant closest to their ideal point. In the table below, consumer (C) at (4, 4) would purchase from restaurant 1 (R1) as it is closet in hedonic space.

In this model (as in the real world), restaurants need sufficient sales to remain in business. I capture this with a threshold for sales, T. If a restaurant does not get at least T consumers, it fails. As the population in the city grows it can support a second restaurant. Where that restaurant locates hedonically will depend on where the first restaurant located. Similarly, where the third restaurant locates will depend on

(Size, Heat)

S/H	1	2	3	4	5	6	7	8	9	10
1		R3								
2										
3						R1				
4				C						
5										
6										
7										
8										
9							R2			
10										

Figure 3.5.

where the first two located. Hence, the final configuration of types of restaurants will depend on the *set* of earlier choices. The outcomes depend on a path of set-dependent actions, so by convention the process is called *path dependent*.

To show formally that this process produces system level diversity, it suffices to prove that, given a distribution of consumers and a threshold, there exist multiple configurations of stable firm locations in hedonic space. A little experimentation with pencil and paper shows this to be true.[39] Different cities will have different configurations of restaurants because their paths of entrants differ. This path dependence creates system level differences.

The multiple configurations arise because payoffs to the restaurants are interdependent—profits depend on finding a niche. Similar intuition can be applied to ecosystems. Species inhabit niches. A niche is a local habitat in which a species can survive. Clearly, niches depend on the behaviors of other species. Therefore, if two ecosystems begin with different species the niches that get constructed down the line likely to differ. Once we include interdependence between diverse types—a hallmark of complex systems—we get the possibility, in fact the likelihood, of diverse configurations.

Creation versus Evolution of Diversity

Until now, I've moved freely between creative systems and evolutionary systems. To conclude this chapter, I highlight differences between the two. In an evolutionary process, the development of new characteristics and attributes occurs through mutation and, in some cases, sexual recombination. Evolution tinkers (Jacob 1977). It has no intentionality, has little inherent bias in search direction, moves slowly, and has no foresight. Evolution wouldn't fail to try something because it *thought* it was unlikely. Nor would it try something because it anticipated that it would be useful in the future. Instead, evolution is a mindless process in which successful mutations and recombinations of genes increase their representations in the population.

Evolution can turn what was a random byproduct into something that adds functionality (Gould and Lewontin 1979). An ear forms from a piece of jaw, and an eye evolves from light-sensitive cells. In contrast, creative processes tend to include intention and intelligence. They are mindful, not mindless. This intelligence has plusses and minuses. Creative processes can take huge leaps. They can anticipate the future. They can also suffer from biases and leap too far or in the wrong direction.

In contrast, evolution relentlessly plods along. The race doesn't always go to the swift. Evolution locates solutions to problems that one would think would only happen in creative systems. This does not mean creative systems don't have some advantages. They do. Creative systems can resurrect ideas from the past. Dinosaurs cannot come back from the dead, but the Volkswagen Beetle was reintroduced when the time was right. I do not mean to imply that evolution has no ability to reach into the past. It can. Some species can become dormant, a process known as *diapause*, and then spring back to life when conditions are right. Populations of some species of beetles form aggregations of tens of thousands of individuals to protect themselves against predators while they're hibernating.

Evolution even has the ability to reach back into the far past, though this takes more time. Stick insects that once had wings have re-evolved those wings. This re-evolution occurs because the developmental pathways remain in place. Some residue of the instructions for the wings remains in the genetic code enabling the species to produce wings anew (Whiting, Bradler, and Maxwell 2003).

Previously, I discussed how creative systems can exploit diverse representations of problems. Another advantage of creative systems is that they can often choose their own selection operator. By that I mean, the creators can decide what gets to reproduce and what does not.[40]

Furthermore, in creative systems, we have the freedom to choose whether to reproduce identically or to experiment. This trade-off between *exploration* and *exploitation* arises often in complex systems (March 1991; Kollman 2003; Miller and Page 2008). It occurs on both fixed and dancing landscapes. On a fixed, rugged landscape problem, such as designing a salad spinner or a particle collider, too much exploitation can result in stopping at a suboptimal solution. Too much exploration can prevent good solutions from being implemented. For example, if I stand before two slot machines at a casino and I'm told that one has a higher expected payoff than the other, I would experiment for a while. Once I thought I had found the better machine, I'd only play it. I'd exploit. If I experimented on the slot machines forever, I wouldn't perform as well as I could. Nor would I do well if I didn't experiment at all.

This balancing between mutation rates and selection also occurs in zero sum games such as the one played between viruses and an immune system. If the virus doesn't mutate, it becomes a fixed target that the immune system can eventually identify. But if the virus mutates too much, it can slide too far from the peak on the landscape and no longer function. This tradeoff makes for a delicate balancing act. In theory, an organism could go extinct because of too much mutation, a phenomenon biologists refer to as *error catastrophe*.

This core logic—that I should explore until it's time to exploit—seems like a compelling solution, but unfortunately it doesn't quite work when the landscapes dance. On dancing landscapes, the peaks change. Returning to the casino example, if the payoffs for the two slot machines change over time, I need to continue to explore at some rate even after I've found the better machine.

Evolutionary systems also have to balance exploration and exploitation. Selection operators do exactly this. A severe selection operator results in over-exploitation. Weak selection or too much mutation may lead to over-exploration. The distinction to note here is that in creative systems, the tradeoff is a matter of choice at each moment in time. Evolutionary systems have evolved a solution to that problem, which may not always work. The flexibility of actors in creative systems to decide how to balance the tradeoff can be seen as an advantage or as just enough slack to cause trouble.

Creative systems have a third advantage. They need not satisfy *interim viability*. By that I mean that each step along the way need not work. In contrast, evolution is constrained in that steps along the path to an improvement must be viable. For example, the four-chambered mammalian heart evolved from a simple tubular heart. Each step along the way, such as the creation of the atrial and ventricular chambers, had to produce a viable entity (see Moorman and Christoffels 2003). Each step need not have produced an increase in fitness per se, but it did have to function.

In creative processes, interim viability is largely irrelevant. Prototypes need not function. In fact, most don't. Attend an auto show, and you will see many car prototypes that are not viable—they lack doors or engines or battery technology. Nevertheless, they serve as templates for further innovation. Evolution has no such luxury. It cannot wait for the four-chambered heart while it continues on evolving other parts of the mammalian body under the expectation that the "heart problem" will be solved by the engineers in the back. The lack of an interim viability requirement enables creative systems to take larger jumps than evolutionary systems. How evolution takes jumps at all has been called the "dilemma of incipient changes" (Gould 1992). In a complex organism with diverse interacting parts, sudden evolution of a new functionality seems unlikely. Darwin's solution to this problem was to distinguish *structural change*, which must be continuous, from *functional change*, which need not be.

A final advantage of creative systems relates to granularity. Owing to technological breakthroughs, creative systems produce increases in the granularity of the basic building blocks. When scientists learned how to break carbon chains, they were then able to produce synthetic motor oil. Synthetic motor oil wasn't possible until the building blocks became sufficiently small. In a 1959 lecture entitled "There's Plenty of Room at the Bottom" Richard Feynman discussed manipulating individual atoms to produce synthetics. The room at the bottom of which he speaks refers to the diversity of possibilities.

The ability to go back in time to exploit a diversity of representations, the choice of selection operators, the lack of an interim viability constraint, and improvements in granularity (not to mention ease of transfer) all suggest that creative systems should be better at producing diversity than evolutionary systems. But that's not necessarily the case. Creative systems can be constrained by cultural blinders. What gets combined and mutated by a creator depends upon the creator's context, her milieu. Ideas that in another time or place may seem obvious may not be considered because they do not belong to the set of ideas that the creator considers.

Take, for example, the anti-coagulant coumadin, a trade name for warfarin. Coumadin must be considered one of the greatest breakthroughs of the past fifty years. The only drug that has saved more lives is penicillin. The history of coumadin merits retelling. Coumadin was developed at the University of Wisconsin in the 1930s after a farmer named

Ed Carlson brought in a dead calf along with some sweet clover that the calf had eaten. A University of Wisconsin scientist, Karl P. Link, discovered that coumarin in the sweet clover was decomposing into dicoumarol, which proved to be an anticoagulant.

Coumadin was a new idea. An idea that could have been transferred to other contexts. How was it transferred? Link's interests tended toward agriculture. So, when he saw an application, it was in that domain. Coumadin's first use was then not to save lives, but as rat poison. It took a couple of decades before coumadin was used to thin human blood and reduce clotting. Cultural blindness—to an agricultural researcher the ability to thin blood suggested the possibility of killing pests, not reducing strokes—limits what ideas get transferred to what contexts.

Whether creative and evolutionary systems are more similar than they are different may not be answerable. At a metaphorical level, many of the processes are similar. Therefore, it is possible to identify core forces for diversity. However, at the mechanistic level, they differ markedly. Those mechanistic differences often matter a great deal and limit our ability to make claims across disciplines. The diversity of memes, products, species, and cultures cannot be wedged into a one-size-fits-all model. That said, this chapter demonstrated that many of the forces that create diversity transcend boundaries. Next, I'll show how the constraints on diversity also apply across contexts.

4

CONSTRAINTS ON DIVERSITY

I don't think things are moving toward an omega point;
I think they're moving toward more diversity.
—CLIFFORD GEERTZ

In this chapter I take up the question of why we see tremendous diversity in some places and not so much in others. For example, why thousands of species of trees but only two species of elephants? Why do rolls of household toilet paper come in one size, while facial tissue is packaged in a range of sizes from larger than a breadbox to smaller than a deck of cards? Why so many species of beetles but a mere fifty or so of rats? And, finally, why so much differentiation in the wood and steel skeletons that support our architectural creations, yet the complete lack of differentiation in the skeletons of mammals?

Some of these questions have straightforward answers. Mammals evolved from common ancestors and were constrained by genetics. And as we learned, structural leaps are not likely. Buildings, which emerge from creative processes, face no such genetic constraints (though they must obey laws of physics). Thus, innovations, such as the move to structural steel construction in taller buildings, need not be incremental, resulting in much greater diversity.

In what follows, I identify constraints—the characteristics or attributes that influence levels of diversity within complex systems. Some of these constraints will be obvious: more space and a greater amount of energy, consumer demand, or biomass make greater diversity possible. Hence, the world supports more types of bacteria and viruses than species of whales, of which there are a few dozen. In formulating these constraints, I rely heavily on complex systems thinking: levels of diversity depend on network structure, rates of adaptation, and interactions. All else equal, systems with fewer connections and higher mutation rates tend to be more diverse, as do systems with moderate levels of interaction.

I focus primarily on diversity of types and not variation or diversity of community composition. This contrasts with the previous chapter, where I devoted substantial attention to variation. There, I needed to include variation given the role it plays in producing type diversity. Here, I'm focusing on constraints on the number of types that can be produced and sustained. Hence, I can largely ignore variation. To keep things simple, I'll rely on the simplest diversity measure: the number of different types.

Nailing down criteria for diversity that transcend context requires a willingness to accept broad generalizations. The characteristics and forces that limit variation within and across ecologies of plants and animals differ in substance from the forces that act within economic, political, or cultural domains. The number of species of mammals hinges upon the size, number, and geographic locations of suitable ecosystems. The number of types of restaurants depends upon the number of consumers and their work lives. These forces, though different in the particulars, still yield to generalization. In each case, the amount of food (species) or demand (economies) plays a major role in determining the level of diversity.

This chapter then provides a flyover of big ideas. For each of these constraints, one can find entire literatures fleshing out the particulars. Economists have models that solve for the equilibrium number of firms as a function of demand, and ecologists have models of the equilibrium number of species. In places, I dig more deeply to flesh out details, such as when I discuss species area laws for ecosystems. But most often, I shoot with a wide lens.

Constraints on Diversity

The first constraint on diversity is the *size of the set of the possible*. The number of possible car designs dwarfs the number of pencil designs. Cars can vary in engine size, number of seats, color, and design. Not all of those cars will sell. That's not my point. The point is that they are possible. A necessary condition for lots of diversity is that it be possible. This first determinant is independent of system thinking. I ignore interactions and adaptations.

To make this constraint formal, I make a strong assumption that entities within whatever category is of interest—be it songbirds or rap songs—can be described using a set of dimensions D, which represent features or variables, and a set of feasible values X_i, $i \in D$ that those features take. If each of X_i has the same number of possible values, that is, the same *cardinality*, say X, then the set of the possible is of size X^D.[41]

Constraint #1: The Size of the Possible X^D, where D = *the dimensionality (the number of distinct features, attributes, or variables) and X = the cardinality (the number of options or values) for each dimension of the defining characteristics of members of the category. The smaller the size of the possible, the less potential for diversity.*

The table below characterizes four extreme cases in the dimensionality/cardinality framework. The high cardinality, high-dimensional box contains a library. Each space on a library shelf can be thought of as a dimension. The cardinality of the set of options for each space in the library equals the number of books in existence, also a huge number. In contrast, while human DNA also has many dimensions, it has low cardinality on each of them. So, DNA goes in the high dimension, low cardinality box. Paints go in the other diagonal box. They have just a few dimensions, including finish (matte, eggshell, flat, satin, etc.) and color, but color has a huge cardinality. In the lower right-hand column I have the letter I. It has really only one dimension and that dimension has a limited cardinality.

The formula X^D can be used to explain why we can have so many more types of houses than types of chairs. The reason: houses have more dimensions. In the formula, dimensionality is in the exponent, so it plays a larger role. A quick example makes the logic clear: 30^2 equals a mere 900, while 2^{30} exceeds a billion. The enormous number of chemical compounds can also be explained using this formula. The number of ways to combine 105 elements is enormous. Of course, not all of these

		Cardinality	
		High	Low
Dimensionality	High	Library	Human DNA
	Low	Paints	the letter *I*

hold together. That's why we have roughly 1.5 million stable compounds and not trillions (Auyang 1998).[42]

The second constraint relates the size of the entity, be it a species or product, to the size of the supporting environment. I refer to this as *relative demand or amount of food*. This requires systems level thinking: the amount of food available depends on actions of other entities, both suppliers of that food and competitors for it. For a species, the analog of demand is niche size. How large is the environment that would support the species? This depends on the available food for that species, which in turn depends on the prevalence of the species itself. These feedback loops imply that relative demand cannot be seen as some exogenous feature, but should instead be thought of as produced by a system.

Constraint #2: Relative Demand or Amount of Food *The size of the niche, level of demand, or amount of food relative to the size of the entity. Decreased relative demand implies less potential diversity.*

The physical size of an object and environments play a role in relative demand: nuclear reactors, aircraft carriers, and elephants have small relative demands; flowers, ants, and Pokeman cards have large relative demands. Of course, physical size doesn't explain everything. Elephants are physically smaller than houses, and their relative demand is also much smaller. To highlight how relative demand gets produced in a system, I offer up a brief aside on what are called species area laws. These relate the number of species to the area available.

Species Area Law, the MacArthur-Wilson Island Model, and Neutral Theory: Empirical ecologists have identified what is called the *species area relationship*. This relates the number of species S to the total land area of an ecosystem A. The relationship can be written as follows:

$$S = CA^z,$$

where C and z are positive constants. For most ecosystems, the exponent z ranges between one fourth and one third. In the case where z equals one fourth, this means that if the area became sixteen times as large, the number of species would double. The species area relationship is an example of a *power law*.[43] Here, because the exponent is positive and less than one, the number of species grows slowly as the area increases.

Note that the equation contains two constants C and z, which means that the number of species of beetles on an island in the West Indies could lie on a different line from the number of frogs in a wetland in the southern United States. What the relationship implies is that both beetles and frogs would lie on straight lines (on log-log paper), but those lines might differ. Thus, if someone discovered a new collection of islands, we could not use the species area law to predict the number of species unless we knew C and z. Those can vary from type of ecosystem to type of ecosystem, so we would be unable to use the species area relationship to make any predictions. However, if we counted the number of species on a subset of the islands, then we could estimate C and z and make accurate predictions for the other islands.

Species area laws are not a theory or a model but an empirical relationship. Their existence led to research on why they hold. One model that relates land area to number of species is the MacArthur-Wilson island model (MacArthur and Wilson 1967). I present a crude version of their model here. The original model was developed to answer the puzzle of why islands had fewer species than inland ecosystems of similar size. The island model has been critiqued, refined, and expanded many times over the years, but the base model gives some intuition for how one might relate number of species and land area. The model relies on two curves: an *extinction curve* and an *immigration curve*. Both curves have the number of species on the horizontal axis.

The *extinction curve* plots the number of species that go extinct, E, as a function of the number of existing species, N. This line is upward sloping. If we don't assume any interdependencies between species, we can assume that this is just a straight line $E = aN$, where a is a positive constant. The *immigration curve* plots the number of new species that arrive, I, as a function of the number of existing species. As this is a model of an island, the farther that island lies from shore, the fewer species that will make their way to the island, and the more horizontal the immigration curve.

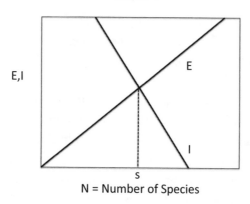

Figure 4.1. Equilibrium diversity in the island model.

This model shows that it's not just the size of the island but also its distance from the shore that determines the amount of diversity. So the second constraint, the relative amount of food, captures one factor: *bigger islands can sustain more species*, but it misses a second factor: *islands further from shore will have fewer species*.

This model proves adequate for predicting the richness (number) of species, but it says little about species abundance—the distribution across types of species. Evidence shows that species distributions typically include few species of large abundance and lots of species with small numbers of members. In other words, most species are rare. An ecologist concerned with preserving species would be wise to concentrate efforts on the long tail of the species distribution—all of those species that exist in small numbers. That requires an understanding of the forces that produce so many species in such small numbers.

In my presentation of these models, I consider the species distribution within a single trophic level. Recall that these are species competing for the same food source. An initial candidate model, MacArthur's Broken Stick Model, conceptualized the food source as a stick of length one. If the trophic level contained N species, then the stick was randomly broken into N segments. This process creates a long tailed distribution that roughly fits some of the early data. For example, in the case where $N = 4$, the species' expected abundances are $\frac{25}{48}$, $\frac{13}{48}$, $\frac{7}{48}$, and $\frac{3}{48}$.

The Broken Stick Model lacks complete micro-foundations. We have no understanding of why allocating the food source like a broken stick makes more sense than allocating it in equal shares. Ideally, we'd have a model that took into account reproduction, death, speciation, and migration. Such a model does exist, the *unified neutral theory of biodiversity*, and it explains species abundance remarkably well (Hubbell 2001). Neutral theory models assume that species at the same trophic level have identical rates of death, birth, migration, and speciation. This means that no species has a selective advantage over any other. The neutral theory contrasts with what Hubbell calls the *niche assembly perspective* which derives the abundance of a species from the species' functionality.

I sketch the preliminaries of the unified neutral model here. I refer the reader to Hubbell's (2001) excellent book for the full treatment. Hubbell originally studied arboreal forests, so I choose trees here as well. Consider a forest consisting of hickories, oaks, elms, and maples. Assume that the forest has exactly 1,000 spots for trees and that if a tree dies, another tree will drop a seed, be it an acorn or a helicopter, to fill it. In the model, trees die at rate d in each period. If a tree dies, assume that another tree is chosen randomly to fill its spot.

Let's add a little math to this story. If there are H_t hickory trees, and with probability d a tree dies, then the probability that a hickory dies equals $d\frac{H_t}{1000}$. If so, there are now $H_t - 1$ hickories. It could be that a new hickory fills the empty location. If so, the number of hickories would be unchanged. But with probability $1 - \frac{H_t-1}{999}$, it will not be a hickory that fills the empty location, and the number of hickories will stay at $H_t - 1$.[44] Putting all of this together, It is possible to write the probability that the number of hickory trees decreases or increases by one in a period.

$$\text{Prob}(H_{t+1} = H_t - 1) = d\frac{H_t}{1000}\left(1 - \frac{H_t - 1}{999}\right)$$

$$= d\frac{H_t(1000 - H_t)}{1000 \cdot 999},$$

$$\text{Prob}(H_{t+1} = H_t + 1) = d\left(1 - \frac{H_t}{1000}\right)\frac{H_t}{999}$$

$$= d\frac{H_t(1000 - H_t)}{1000 \cdot 999}.$$

Note that these two probabilities are the same. This means that the number of hickory trees can be modeled as a random walk with mean zero. If I start with some allocation of 1,000 trees, say 340 hickories, 400 oaks, 100 elms, and 160 maples, then, over time, the numbers of each type of tree will move up and down. Notice that the system keeps churning, but only for a while. Eventually the forest will have only a single type of tree. And once it reaches this state, it will remain in that state forever. In forests with lots of trees, the time to convergence for this model will be long.

To prevent monocultures from arising in the model, new species must arise. This could occur through in-migration or through speciation. In the unified neutral model, in-migration can be included by introducing a rate at which neighboring species enter the ecosystem. If a vast oak forest lies to the west of our model forest, then the in-migration rate of oaks would be high, and, in the long run, our forest would contain lots of oaks. Thus, the prevalence of a species will depend on its in-migration rate.

Now, all that is left to do in this model is to add speciation. In constructing models, often simplest is best. That's true here as well. Hubbell (2001) assumes a constant rate of speciation. With some small probability, a hickory tree spreads a rogue seed producing a new species. That probability is the same for all types of trees. New species will not be that likely to spread because the probability of filling an open spot is proportional to the number of members of that species. This feature of the model produces distributions within which rare species are prevalent.

The unified neutral theory is not universally accepted even though it proves able to produce accurate explanations of species abundance distributions. Here, I care less about the academic debates than I do about the following method-ological point: the unified neutral theory shows that we can construct a model that produces nontrivial distributions of species richness (number of types) and species abundance (distributions across those types). The same might be done in other disciplines in which distributions of types play a less central role. In addition, the simplicity of the neutral theory allows for extensions. In the unified neutral theory presented here, the action takes place on a single island. It's possible, though not easy, to add more islands and to position them in geographic space. Doing so allows scientists to make predictions about spatial patterns of species and makes the predictions more specific and more complete. Economo and Keitt (2008) construct one such example.

The third constraint concerns interdependencies and co-ordination constraints. Building bricks have to coordinate with one another, but not as much power cords or water hoses. Coordination reduces diversity, as do other interde-pendencies between different types: the legs of bees that move pollen from flower to flower must be sticky enough to collect pollen, but not so sticky that the pollen cannot rub off onto neighboring flowers. Similarly, the proboscis of a moth must be of appropriate length to drink the nectar from a flower. This constrains the set of possible lengths that can survive in the population of moths. In complex systems, the amount of interdependence and coordination required can change over time as entities adapt to one another.

Constraint #3: Interdependence/Coordination *The necessity of coordination with similar types and the amount of inter-dependence with other types for success or survival. Greater interdependence reduces the amount of diversity.*

Interdependence and coordination occur within both species and products. Given the mammalian brain's many functions, its various parts cannot evolve independently of one another. Yet, this does not mean that the evolution must occur in lockstep. Different parts of the brain can grow at different rates during the evolutionary process. These differential rates of change are referred to as *mosaic evolution* (Barton and Harvey 2000). Mosaic evolution enables change in systems with lots of interdependencies.

To see the importance of interdependence and coordination on levels of diversity, consider two cases: books and computer operating systems. In a given year, more than a quarter million books are published in the United States alone. The set of the possible is enormous. Relative demand is high, and constraints imposed by coordination and interdependencies are minimal. A new cookbook is not affected in any meaningful way by thousands of new self-help books, mysteries, or books on statistics. In contrast, consider the market for computer operating systems. These also have a huge set of the possible and high demand, but coordination effects reduce the number of viable systems to a mere handful.

At this point, many readers may sense a contradiction. Recall that in the previous chapter I argued that coordination can be a cause of diversity. Here, I'm arguing that it's a constraint. Both are true. There I demonstrated how coordination within a community can create diversity across communities. Here, I am suggesting that the requirements to coordinate within a community reduce diversity within that community. That is true as well. The same logic holds for ecosystems. Coupled landscapes limit what occurs within an ecosystem but are an engine of diversity across ecosystems.

The fourth constraint on diversity concerns the variation of selective pressures; by this I mean whether selective pressures always point in the same or different directions. If there is no variation in selective pressure, then in the long run only one type will survive. If selection pressures vary over time, then more types can exist. Note that this constraint has the same flavor as the interim disturbance hypothesis, which is an empirical regularity and which we saw hold provided we add assumptions like populations dependent fitness or physical space.

Constraint #4: Variation of Selection *The variation in selective pressures on different dimensions. Less variation in selective pressure results in less diversity.*

This constraint can help us understand the lack of diversity in oil tankers. Selective pressure arises from profit considerations. Bigger oil tankers are more cost effective. Volume increases much faster than surface area, so construction costs fall markedly per unit of volume. The width of canals limits their size, so selection drives out all but the largest possible tankers.

If we constructed a toy model of selection with a single fitness function, we would expect to see a single type. Ecologists refer to this as the principle of *competitive exclusion.* In real ecosystems and in markets, selection operates on multiple dimensions and the weights on those dimensions vary, so pure competitive exclusion is rare. The fitness of a maple or oak tree depends on the robustness of its seedlings and on its method of seed dispersal. Multiple species that compete for a common resource can coexist provided each has some advantage for one of the selective pressures. Selection may sometimes favor the sturdy acorn and sometimes favor the maple's disperse, auto rotating helicopters. Similarly, in the market for chairs, selection occurs on price, quality, comfort, durability, and style. As a result, the market supports lots of types of chairs.

The next constraint considers functionality. It's one thing to say that you could make broccoli ice cream and biodegradable tofu car seats, and another thing altogether to say that either could survive in the marketplace. I also refer to this as a brittleness constraint. Human DNA is highly brittle. A random string of human length DNA would not produce a viable child. Medicines are also brittle—any small changes to their molecular composition and they stop working. For example, of all the possible ways to make insulin, at present only seventeen function. Brittleness tends to correlate with complicatedness. Brass paperweights are not at all brittle, nor are beanbags, but computer software often is.

Constraint #5: Functionality/Brittleness *Whether a member of the set of the possible is functional or can survive. Greater brittleness implies less diversity.*

The functionality constraint applies not just to physical characteristics, but also to performance attributes. Consumers would flock to buy a car that got six hundred miles to the gallon, went from zero to sixty in five seconds, and seated seven. But such cars, for the moment, do not exist. In the biological world, functionality constraints are often physical. In his classic book, *On Growth and Form*, D'Arcy Thompson (1992) shows that the theoretical maximal leaping height is independent of scale across species of the same shape. That doesn't mean that fleas, frogs, people, horses, and cheetahs can all jump equally high. (Cheetahs can clear 15 feet.) It means that if we built a two-inch tall human, she'd jump six feet high. A frog that jumps forty feet high would violate laws of physics.[45]

Evolution may also drive structural and functional characteristic to an efficient frontier. The metabolism of species scales with body size on an almost perfect line on a log linear plot (West et al. 1997). And the ratio of white matter (connections) to gray matter (neurons) in the brain is invariant to species size. This makes sense if we think of the brain as a network of small computers. In such a network, the ratio of communication to computation should be relatively constant. If the number of neurons far outstrips the information getting to them, they would have nothing to do. Conversely, if too much information gets to the neurons, they would be overloaded (Brown and West 2000).

Other functional constraints explain variations in life expectancy. The number of heartbeats in a lifetime appears to be invariant to size. The mouse and the elephant get the same number of beats. As do humans. That number is about 2.6 billion. Similar constraints may well hold in social systems——some features of firms and organizations may be constrained by efficiency considerations such as amount of time and resources spent on hiring in organizations.

The flip side holds as well: a lack of functionality constraints produces abundant diversity. Petroski (1992) counts five million patents. Patents need only be new ideas. We have an abundance of patents because they face few selective pressures other than functionality. If an idea works, it can be patented. As a result, patents have been awarded for some pretty crazy things that probably won't survive in the marketplace. Patents in the category of socks include moisturizing socks, socks that have pockets, inflatable socks, and tap dance socks (Chartand 2000). Ideas can run contrary to theory and still receive patents. Hence, the number of patents for perpetual motion machines exceeds zero and would be much larger had not the U.S. Patent Office in 1911 begun requiring that any perpetual motion machine must run for an entire year prior to being granted a patent (Lemonick 2000).

The final constraint is plasticity or the ability to explore the set of the possible. Think back to the MacArthur-Wilson island model. The amount of diversity depended on the rate of immigration. Immigration is a proxy for plasticity. The level of plasticity depends on characteristics of system. The first is the ease with which an innovator can maneuver in the space of the possible, in other words, the rate of adaptation.

Constraint #6: Plasticity and Rate of Adaptation *The ability of entities in the system to explore new functional possibilities, and the rate at which those explorations occur.*

Plasticity seems like a great idea. Species that can adapt to changing circumstances would seem to have a reproductive advantage. True enough, but adaptability comes at a cost. Strawberries can alter their chemistry to adapt to changing light, but photosynthetic flexibility requires extra sensory apparatus (Levin 2000).

Creative systems have amazing plasticity and therefore lots of diversity. Beinhocker (2006) estimates that world markets support on the order of ten billion stock keeping units (SKUs). SKUs uniquely identify a type of product. They're familiar to us as the bar codes we see on packages. That's more than one product for each person who ever lived.

Finally, the amount of plasticity depends on the extent to which exploration has limited range. In computer science, a search is referred to as *local* if it only changes a small number of attributes or features. If innovations must be near existing entities, then diversity will be limited. The extent to which search is local depends on the process that produces variation. In asexual reproduction, variation comes solely from mutation and is therefore quite limited. In architecture, it's possible for someone to design anything—witness Frank Gehry's Guggenheim museum in Bilbao and Walt Disney Concert Hall in Los Angeles. Even though anything could be possible (subject to physical constraints), architects are often quite conservative. They're hemmed in by cultural constraints as discussed in the previous chapter.

Applying the Constraints

The constraints can be applied to any category to predict whether we would expect a high or low diversity of types. As a test, consider the diversity of types of bricks, snakes, and children's toys. I'll start with bricks. The number of possible bricks is high. Demand for bricks is substantial, and bricks aren't especially brittle. These constraints suggest lots of diversity. In the table below, I assign a plus sign (+) next to each of these constraints for bricks. However, bricks must coordinate with one another and with other building materials. They have a only a few dimensions of selection and not a great deal of variation of selective forces on those dimensions. Furthermore, the rate of search for new types of bricks isn't very high. For each of these constraints, I assign a minus sign ($-$). Aggregating the pluses and minuses implies that bricks should be moderately diverse, which is empirically the case; a typical brick manufacturer offers five or six dozen types of bricks.[46] Worldwide, I estimate a few thousand types of bricks.

For both children's toys and snakes, the set of the possible would also be large. Toys have an especially large set of the possible, so I place a plus ($+$) under toys for number possible. The relative demand or niche-to-size ratio for children's toys is also enormous. Children like toys. Grandparents love to buy toys for them. Once again, toys get a plus. The analog of the relative demand for snakes is size of the niches in ecosystems that support them. Snakes are carnivorous and live in deserts as well as tropical rainforests. This points in the direction of lots of types of snakes. But snakes are also prey for large mammals, predatory birds, and humans, and human population growth crowds out snakes. Averaging all these contributions probably produces a net effect of approximately zero.

Snakes need to coordinate with other species in their ecosystems. They must be able to catch and digest their prey and avoid their predators. Snakes have an abundance of possible food sources. Therefore, snakes get a zero (0) for the interactions constraint. Children's toys get a plus. While they have some interactions—train tracks and construction blocks work best if they are of identical scale—most children's toys can function in isolation.

Snakes have relatively little variation in the selective pressures. They must be quick and strong enough to catch their prey, they must be elusive or camouflaged to hide from their predators, and they must be able to withstand climatic variations. Therefore, they get a minus in that column. Children's toys, on the other hand, have lots of variation in their selective forces. Children differ in the colors they like and in the animals they prefer. Some kids like trucks, others like dolls, and many like both. Demand is diverse because children are diverse in their interests. The people who buy gifts for children also have different aims. Some want to be liked, others want to provide economic assistance, and others want to encourage mental development. This diversity of intent also translates into greater diversity in toys. Therefore, children's toys again get a plus.

Functionality constraints on snakes are also fairly high, but not so for children's toys. McDonald's, the largest distributor of toys in the United States, includes some toys in its happy meals that appear to be random collections of parts. Yet, children derive enjoyment from them. Therefore, I assign a minus to snakes and a plus to children's toys on the brittleness constraint. Finally, on the rate of search constraint, snakes rely on evolution to create new species. Evolution has had a long time to evolve snake species. So, on balance, I assign a zero to snakes on the constraint. Children's toys can be produced quickly at low cost. This is why you can buy more types of toy cars than real cars. Years are required to bring a real car from concept to production. Factories must be retooled, and subcontractors must be found to manufacture the thousands of individual parts that make up a car. For a typical die cast metal toy car, the process can be started and completed in a matter of weeks. A tool and die maker creates a mold; the cars are stamped, painted, packaged, and sold. Children's toys again earn a plus.

Constraint	Bricks	Snakes	Toys
Number Possible	+	+	+
Relative Demand	+	0	+
Interactions	−	0	+
Variance of Selection	−	−	+
Functionality/Brittleness	+	−	+
Rate of Search	−	0	+

The plus minus system of accounting is imprecise and ignores the interplay between the constraints. Nevertheless, the analysis performs satisfactorily. It implies that we should see only modest diversity of snakes, the same magnitude, perhaps, that we saw in bricks. This turns out to be the case. Scientists have identified fewer than three thousand snake species. The constraints imply that we should see an amazing diversity of toys. And we do.

As shown in this chapter, to explain the amount of diversity present in a particular system, we must think from a systems perspective. Only one of the six constraints of diversity—*the size of the possible*—can be considered outside the context of a system. *Relative demand, interactions, variation of selection, functionality,* and *rate of adaptation* are all system level properties. Therefore, the amount of diversity that we see within any complex system depends on the other characteristics of that system—the connectedness, the network of patterns of those connections, the rate of adaptation, and so on. The characteristics of the system—how fast other entities adapt, the extent of interdependencies, and the size of niches—all affect the amount of diversity we see.

5

VARIATION IN COMPLEX SYSTEMS

Every case of extinction of a species is a failure to provide
any variations which could have been used to meet and
overcome the circumstances which were leading the
species downhill.
—H.G. WELLS, JULIAN HUXLEY, AND G.P. WELLS,
THE SCIENCE OF LIFE, 1930, P. 415

In this chapter I focus on the roles that variation plays in
complex systems. Prior to taking on that topic, I provide
some scaffolding for what's to follow. One of my main
points will be that variation enhances system level robustness.
Therefore, it's necessary first to clarify the concept of
robustness and to distinguish it from stability. Robustness is
often not given the depth of analysis it deserves. Here I do
not attempt a comprehensive survey of the literature on the
topic (see Jen 2005; Levin 2000; Krakauer 2005): I simply
get a few of the main ideas out on the table.

I then explore the impact of variation through three
simple models. The first model considers the tradeoff
between exploration and exploitation on a fixed, rugged

landscape. This model doesn't include interactions between the members of the same type, which I take on second. When members of a type interact, variation can be stabilizing or destabilizing depending on whether the feedbacks between actions are negative or positive. In systems with negative feedbacks, variation moderates the effects of shocks, but in systems with positive feedbacks, variation can produce tips. In the final model, increases in variation signal a looming phase transition. In that model, variation allows the system to innovate, to move to a new and better solution.

Robustness: An Overview

One of the more active research areas in complex systems investigates robustness (Jen 2005). Robustness has many definitions (Krakauer 2005). Jen defines robustness as the ability of a system to maintain functionality in the face of some change or disturbance, which could be internal or external to the system. The nature of those changes and disturbances depends on the system under study. In a biological system, genetic mutations are a disturbance. In an ecology, disturbances involve the extinction of old species, so called "knockouts", and the invasion of new ones.

As I mentioned in my brief summary of the diversity-stability debate, robustness is not the same thing as stability (Jen 2005). Stability refers to the tendency of a system to return to an equilibrium given a dynamic. A ball at rest at the bottom of a bowl is stable. Give the ball a little push, and it will roll around but quickly return to the same equilibrium. In contrast, robustness refers to the capability of a system to continue to perform in diverse circumstances.

The key point to keep in mind is that a robust system need not go back to the same equilibrium. A human's psyche can be robust if it can survive difficult circumstances. A person's psyche will be permanently changed as the result of a major event like the birth of a child. It won't, like the ball in the bowl, go to the same spot. Yet, the person will still function (Stearns 1998). Robustness can also be applied to political systems. A federal system of government that has redundant, complementary safeguards will be more robust than one that relies on a single institution to right itself (Bednar 2009).

Robust systems must respond to changing circumstances without failing. Typically, we think of robustness in terms of responses to trauma, but a system must also be robust to beneficial changes. For example, a family may or may not be robust to winning the lottery. The increase in wealth could give individual members new opportunities that they prefer to pursue alone.

The concept of robustness captures day-to-day sustainability as well as responsiveness to shocks. Thus, as used here, it expands on the notion of *resilience*, which considers the ability of a system to respond to and recover from trauma (Holling 1973). Note also that robustness can apply to both systems and the entities that comprise those systems.

The concept of robustness can apply on multiple time scales. To biologists, a robust species is one that survives through many geologic eras (Erwin 2001). The sandhill crane, which has a continuous fossil record of over 2.5 million years, would satisfy this definition of robust.

Robustness can also be considered in much shorter time frames. Doctors think in terms of the here and now. A robust physical constitution is one that can withstand viruses, changes in diet, and exposure to harmful chemicals. Biologists also care about short-term robustness, such as whether a species can survive a drought or hurricane. Social scientists take into account both time scales as well when they characterize robustness. Political systems must be able to cope with immediate threats, such as war, as well as drifts caused by changing demographics and technologies (Bednar 2009).

The Exploration-Exploitation Tradeoff

I now turn to the question of how variation contributes to system level robustness using some relatively simple models. First, I show how variation can be interpreted as a kind of search, and how that improves responsiveness when the landscape dances. For example, in trying to find a solution to a problem, say designing a vacuum cleaner or an aardvark, both exploration and exploitation occur. Innovation requires exploring the space of possibilities, but at some point exploration must stop. It's costly, and at some point what has been learned must be exploited. Otherwise, we'd never get anywhere. Thus, ideally, a system would initially have lots of diversity, but then eventually reduce it. This idea underpins a process called simulated annealing, which has a schedule for reducing the amount of diversity over time (Miller and Page 2008).

Fisher's Theorem and the Price Equation

A good place to begin thinking about variation and search is Fisher's (1930) theorem of natural selection. This theorem relates the rate of increase in fitness of an organism to its genetic variance. An example reveals the logic of Fisher's theorem. In this example, I assume two populations of sixty turtles each. These turtles vary in their speeds. In the first population (Pop1), twenty turtles have a top speed of three miles per hour (mph), twenty have a top speed of four mph, and twenty have a top speed of five mph. In the second population (Pop2), the speeds have greater variance, with twelve turtles topping out at speeds two, three, four, five, and six miles per hour. For the moment, I equate fitness with top speed so that average fitness in each population equals four. To simplify the presentation, I let N_s be the number of turtles with a top speed of s miles per hour.

Pop1: $N_3 = 20$, $N_4 = 20$, and $N_5 = 20$

Pop2: $N_2 = 12$, $N_3 = 12$, $N_4 = 12$, $N_5 = 12$, and $N_6 = 12$

To explain the dynamics, I return to the *replicator equation*:

$$p_i^{t+1} = p_i^t \frac{\pi_i}{\bar{\pi}^t}.$$

This equation gives the proportion of type i at time $t+1$, p_i^{t+1}, as a function of the proportion at time t, p_i^t, and the ratio of the fitness of that type, π_i, relative to the average fitness at time t, $\bar{\pi}^t$. Here, there will be two differences between how we interpret the earlier replicator equation and this one. Previously, the i's indexed distinct types: turtles, frogs, bees, etc. Here, they denote variants within the same type: turtles. Second, here we're using numbers, not proportions, so the rule will be written as

$$N_i^{t+1} = N_i^t \frac{\pi_i}{\bar{\pi}^t},$$

where the Ns denote numbers instead of proportions. In this equation, the number of turtles with a top speed of three mph in the first population will equal the number of turtles with that top speed times the ratio of their fitness to average fitness, or 20 times $\frac{3}{4}$, which equals fifteen. Similar calculations show that the populations in the next generation look as follows:

Pop1: $N_3 = 15$, $N_4 = 20$, and $N_5 = 25$,
Average Speed: $4\frac{1}{6}$

Pop2: $N_2 = 6$, $N_3 = 9$, $N_4 = 12$, $N_5 = 15$, and $N_6 = 18$,
Average Speed: $4\frac{1}{3}$

Pop2, which had higher variance in speeds, ends up with a higher fitness in the next period. This example can be generalized into Fisher's theorem, which is most easily derived as a special case of the *Price equation*. The Price equation applies to a population of entities. These could be beetles, sunflowers, or auto companies. These entities differ in the amount of some characteristic that they possess. In other words, they exhibit variation along this characteristic.

It's possible to partition the population into sets that have the same amount of the characteristic. For example, everyone in set i would have the same speed or the same height. Given that partitioning, the Price equation characterizes the change in average fitness, exploiting the fact that the proportions in a set are given by the replicator equation. The Price equation shows how the amount of the characteristic in set i in the next time period can change due to crossover and mutation. Thus, the offspring of the turtles with speed five mph might not have an average speed of five mph. The Price equation captures these changes as well as the changes in fitness that result from replication to give the total change in the amount of the characteristic.[47]

Fisher's Theorem and the Price Equation

Partition a population of size N into K sets so that the members of set i all have the same amount z_i of some attribute θ. Let p_i denote the proportion of the population in set i. It follows that the expected amount of the attribute equals $\bar{z} = \sum_{i=1}^{K} p_i z_i$. Let π_i denote the fitness of the members of set i and $\bar{\pi}$ denote average fitness. Finally, let Δz_i denote the change in the amount of attribute θ among the descendants of the members of set i. The change in the average amount of the attribute θ is given by the equation

$$\Delta \bar{z} = \sum_{i=1}^{K} \left[p_i \frac{\pi_i}{\bar{\pi}} (z_i + \Delta z_i) - p_i z_i \right]$$

Rearranging terms gives

$$\bar{\pi} \Delta \bar{z} = \sum_{i=1}^{K} [p_i \pi_i z_i - \bar{\pi} p_i z_i + p_i \pi_i \Delta z_i]$$

$$= \sum_{i=1}^{K} [p_i \pi_i z_i] - \bar{\pi} \bar{z} + E[\pi \Delta z]$$

This yields the **Price Equation:**

$$\bar{\pi} \Delta \bar{z} = \text{Cov}[\pi, z] + E[\pi \Delta z],$$

where $\text{Cov}[\pi, z]$ equals the covariance of π and z. In the special case, where the characteristic θ is fitness

$(z = \pi)$, if we ignore changes in fitness due to mutations so that $\Delta z = 0$, we get **Fisher's Fundamental Theorem:**

$$\bar{\pi}\,\Delta\bar{\pi} = \mathrm{Var}[\pi],$$

which says that the change in fitness ($\Delta\bar{\pi}$) equals the variance.

The first term in the Price equation states that the change in the average fitness depends on the covariance of the attribute θ (recall this is what z measures) and fitness.[48] This makes intuitive sense. More variance implies more high fitness offspring (that get produced with higher probability) and more low fitness offspring (that get produced with lower probability). The second term captures the change in the levels of the attribute within each set (the Δz_i terms). The Price equation tells us exactly how much of an attribute will exist in the population in the next period. If we let the attribute equal fitness itself, then we get Fisher's theorem.

The idea that fitness increases with variance proves useful as a departure point for thinking about variation as a form of search. This logic can be made more formal (Weitzman 1979). Suppose that you're moving to a new town or city and you have an afternoon to check out the housing market and find a house to buy. You have time to visit some fixed number of houses, say eight. Your goal is to find the best possible house. Consider two different search strategies—one that is high variance and one that's much safer.[49] The high variance approach might be driving around and looking at any houses you see for sale. The low variance approach would be to consult a real estate agent and look at houses in your price range.

For the purposes of this example, we can abstract away from the notion of a landscape and instead consider the value of a house as a draw from a distribution. In this way, I can capture the high variance search strategy as draws from a distribution H that has a large variance and the low variance search strategy as draws from a distribution L that has a low variance. I will assume that L has a higher mean value than H, but that H has longer tails in each direction. By that I mean that H will result in more low values and more high values. As shown in the box below, as the number of searches increases, what determines the value of the best solution found is weight in the upper tail of the distribution. Therefore, if you have time to look at enough houses, drawing from H becomes the better choice even though it has a lower mean value.

Search for the Best: The Value of the Tail

Given a cumulative distribution function F, let $\mu(F) = \int x \, dF(x)$ denote the expected value of a single draw from the distribution F and $\mu^k(F) = \int kx F^{(k-1)}(x) dF(x)$ denote the expected value of the best of k draws.

The Value of the Tail: *Let $L(x)$ and $H(x)$ be two cumulative distribution functions that satisfy (i) $\mu(L) > \mu(H)$; and (ii) there exists a T such that $H(T) < L(T) = 1$. Then there exist a number of searches K such that for any $k > K$, searching from H has a higher best value, i.e., $\mu^k(H) > \mu^k(L)$.*

Example: L is a uniform distribution on $[8, 9]$ and H is a uniform distribution on $[0, 10]$. Then

$\mu^k(L) = 8 + \frac{k}{k+1} = \frac{9k+8}{k+1}$ and $\mu^k(H) = \frac{10k}{k+1}$.
Therefore, $\mu^k(H) > \mu^k(L)$ if and only if $10k > 9k+8$, or $k > 8$.

Note that the first condition, that the expected value from a single draw of L exceeds the expected value of a single draw from H, is not needed for the proof. However, without that assumption the result isn't surprising. If H had a higher mean, it would be a better distribution to draw from.

Now that we have the basic intuition that higher variance implies more high value solutions, it's useful to return to the idea of a landscape and to reconsider the question of how to balance exploration (where variation is good) and exploitation. On a fixed landscape, once a good solution is located, variance would no longer be a good thing. Variation would lower fitness and profits. Deviations in beak size or in the amount of sugar in a can of soda would represent slippage from the peak. But our focus here is not on fixed landscapes. In a complex system, the value or fitness of a solution depends on the actions of other entities in the system. The landscape dances.

When a landscape dances, local peaks can change. What used to be locally optimal may no longer be a peak, what was slippage on a fixed landscape will be exploration on a dancing landscape. As an example, suppose that pollution from coal-fired plants darkens buildings and trees. The optimal shading for moths that hide on the bark of trees will now be a little darker. If the initial population of moths had sufficient variation, some of the initial population that was too dark may now be exactly the right color.

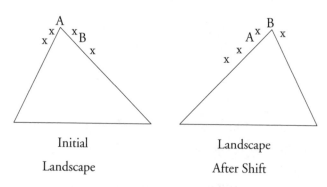

Initial

Landscape

Landscape

After Shift

Figure 5.1. Initial and After Shift Landscape.

Pictures similar to those used to explain the evolution of diversity clarify this intuition. In the initial landscape, A is at the peak and B is suboptimal. After the shift in the landscape, B becomes optimal.

If I add selection to this model, over time, selection would center the population at the peak. After the shift in the landscape, most members of the population would be to the left of peak A. But those farthest to the left would be least likely to reproduce, as they have lowest fitness. This would truncate the variation to the left. Those lying to the right of the peak have relatively high fitness. Therefore, they'd be more likely to reproduce, which would rebalance the population around the new peak.

The Optimal Level of Variation in a Complex System: The analysis so far points to an interesting question: how much variation should a population maintain? The answer depends partly on how often the landscape shifts, and by how much. Again, a simple model is useful. Imagine a one-dimensional attribute, such as the beak length of finches. Let Θ_t denote the optimal beak length at time t. This is the peak on the landscape. Assume that optimal beak length follows a random walk.[50] In one year, the optimal beak length might be 3.4 cm. The next year it might be 3.5 cm.

Now, suppose that the finches had no variation in the length of their beaks. Then only rarely would their beak length be optimal. Alternatively, suppose that the variation within the population was enormous. This would guarantee some finches with optimal beak lengths, but it would also mean that many finches would have beaks that were far too short or far too long. The optimal amount of variation from year to year depends on the speed of the random walk. If the random walk takes large jumps, then the variation within the population should be large so that the population can find the new peak. If the steps in the random walk tend to be small, then the variation should also be small.

This insight—that the level of variation should track the rate of disturbances—leads to the question: can an entity within a complex system locate this optimal level of variation? Yes. In fact, it's relatively easy. To see how, we can return to our landscape model and think of the level of variation as the feature that adapts. Given a rate of disturbance, there exists an optimal level of variation. Except in rare cases, the closer the level of variation is to the optimal level, the better the population will perform on average. Therefore, the "variation landscape" isn't rugged. It's single-peaked, and easily scaled.

In working through this logic, I've taken the rate of disturbances as exogenous—as occurring outside the system. In complex systems, the rate of disturbance to a landscape would be endogenous—it would depend on how fast other entities adapt and respond. Therefore, it would also depend on the levels of variation in other species. Whether levels of variation settle down or vary over time depends on the complex system and the path it takes. In either case, what's important to keep in mind is that for any type of entity, the appropriate level of variation will eventually emerge from the system. Moreover, that level will tend to track the rate at which the system churns.

Variation and Stability: Interactions and Feedbacks

So far, I have interpreted the members of a population as solutions to a problem: products that have a value, policies that have an efficiency, or species that have a fitness. The members of a population have not interacted with one another. I now consider the possibility that the entities interact. I restrict attention to two types of interactions: *negative feedbacks* and *positive feedbacks*. I demonstrate how in systems with negative feedbacks, variation produces stability, and in systems with positive feedbacks, variation can make systems more prone to tip.[51]

A *negative feedback* exists when increases in the propensity of an action decrease the benefits from taking that action. For example, people like to go to the beach on Saturdays, but as the beach gets more crowded, it becomes less attractive. I want to expand on this crude intuition with a model to show how variation creates not robustness but stability. Consider a simple model of beach attendance with one thousand people. Each person has a threshold T, and goes to the beach on Saturday if fewer than T people went to the beach the previous Saturday. Set a common threshold, $T = 400$, for everyone. Suppose 300 people go to the beach on the first Saturday. The second Saturday all 1,000 people will go because attendance the first week was below the threshold. Given that 1,000 people went the second week, no one will go the third week. Given that no one went the third week, everyone will go the fourth week, and so on and so on. The result will be a volatile swing in which everyone goes one week and no one the next.

Now, of course, people are smarter than this, and this situation wouldn't happen, but bees are not. Bees face a problem that's similar to the beach problem. They want to maintain a comfortable temperature in the hive. Bees have an internal mechanism that determines when the hive is too hot or too cold. When it's too hot, they fan out. When it's too cool, they huddle together. A hive of genetically identical bees will all get hot and cold at the same temperature. The result will be just like that in our beach model. The hive gets too hot, so the bees all fan out and cool the hive. But then the hive gets too cool, so they huddle together, which causes the hive to get too hot.

If the bees have different temperatures at which they get hot and cold, that is, if they have variance in their temperature thresholds, then these fluctuations become less severe. Suppose that the hive's temperature begins to rise. Now, unlike before, not all of the bees will feel the need to fan the hive—only a few will. Those few will fan out and reduce the temperature until some of them begin to feel comfortable, at which point those bees will stop fanning and the temperature will equilibrate (Jones et al. 2004).

The toy model of the beach and the real world example of the bees shows how variation promotes stability when negative feedbacks are present. With positive feedbacks, the opposite occurs: variation in thresholds leads to an increase in the probability of large events. This observation can be made more formal with Granovetter's (1978) riot model. Imagine that a group of people are milling around during a time of social upheaval, and each individual in the group is trying to decide whether to riot. As in the beach model, each person has a threshold, only now this threshold determines whether a person begins to riot.

By comparing two scenarios, I can show how variation leads to big events. In the first, each of one thousand people has a threshold of twenty. Any person who sees at least twenty people rioting will join the riot. The result of this distribution of thresholds will be that no riot occurs. In the second scenario, assume that ten people have threshold zero, ten people have threshold ten, ten have threshold twenty, ten have threshold thirty, and so on. This crowd of people is not nearly as angry as the first crowd. Their average threshold is approximately five hundred. And yet, in this scenario, a riot erupts. This is because, initially, ten people riot (those with threshold zero), and then ten more do, and so on, and so on. The variation in thresholds allows the system to tip.

For this reason—variation in thresholds creating tipping points—predicting the timing of riots is notoriously difficult. The fall of the Berlin Wall between East and West Germany might have been expected, given economic performance and levels of discontent in the East, but no one could have guessed exactly when it would take place (Lohmann 1994). We also could not predict its speed once it began: the fall of eastern Europe happened quickly. Once riots began, the distribution of thresholds (and information) was such that the unrest spread like wildfire.

Variation as a Signal

Variation can also act as a signal in complex systems. Consider an ecological system that is undergoing a phase transition, such as a lake becoming eutrophic or a grassland moving toward desertification. During the phase transition, the fitness landscape for species will shift. That shift in the landscape may transform what was a peak into a flat spot on the fitness landscape. This implies the potential for an increase in variation prior to a major change in the system.

This phenomenon of increasing variation is shown in Figure 5.2. In the first frame, the members of the species show moderate variation near the peak on the fitness landscape 5.2(a). As the systems near a phase transition, the fitness landscape becomes less steep near that peak. As a result, the amount of selective pressure to be near the peak declines and variation increases as shown in 5.2(b). This increase in variation signals the upcoming phase transition and enables the species to locates the new peak 5.2(c).

This insight holds more generally. We should expect the amount of variation on a trait to be higher when systems are in flux and lower when they are stable. When ecosystems are in flux, selective pressures won't all point to the same solution producing more variation. Economies work this way as well. When fashion trends are in flux, we should see

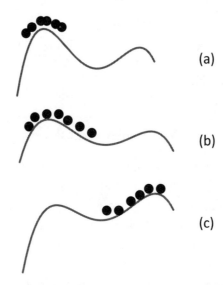

Figure 5.2. Increase in variation prior to phase transition.

more variation in the length of skirts and width of ties than when the system is stable. On the one hand, this insight is obvious—if a system hasn't settled down, there must be more variation. On the other hand, it is very deep: If a system is about to undergo a shift, once-stable configurations may have difficulty holding together, resulting in more variation.

One last point related to figure 5.2. Notice that the increase in variation prior to the phase transition also allows the new peak to be located. This points to the connection between variation and robustness. Therefore, in the example, variation plays two roles: as a local peak becomes less steep, variation increases, signaling the possibility of a phase transition. Once that phase transition occurs, the same variability allows the population to locate a new peak. The variation enables innovation that leads to the new solution that produces a robust system.

Variation and Robustness: Incentives and Foresight

Variation need not always improve robustness. A core question in international relations is the extent to which variation in power promotes system level robustness. Note that when international relations scholars refer to *stable* regimes, they do not mean that any perturbation will return the system to its initial state; what they mean is that the primary players and alliances will not change. Therefore, what they mean lies on the boundary between what I call stable (the same equilibrium) and robust (maintenance of functionality). So I will refer to the robustness of the political system, and not its stability.

The idea of a balance of power dates back at least to Thomas Hobbes (1660) and probably to the Greeks. Balance of power theory, in its crudest form, states that if two actors have equal power, the system will be robust. Those two actors could be individual states or alliances. In either case, with power being relatively equal neither actor is likely to challenge the other. However, if there is variation in power, the system may not be robust, as one actor may have an incentive to attack the other.[52]

In addition to the two actors having equal power, it helps that they have accurate beliefs about their relative power. If one actor believes itself to be stronger, it might well attack. My point here is a simple one: in cases of potential conflict, a lack of variation can promote robustness. Therefore, it's not correct to say that more variation always leads to greater robustness.

Summary: Variation or Diversity?

In this chapter, I have discussed relationships between variation and the functionality of complex systems. More variation isn't necessarily better, as shown in the tradeoff between exploration and exploitation. What is true is that some variation is necessary for a complex system to maintain functionality. Variation within a type of entity allows the entire system to respond to changing circumstances.

Throughout the chapter, I have focused on variation. A closer look at the examples shows that in many, the line between variation, differences within a type, and diversity, differences across types, was rather blurry. For example, in the threshold model of riots, the variation in thresholds for individuals probably results from underlying diversity—differences in life experiences, beliefs, or mental models.

What I have called "variation in thresholds" captures a deeper diversity of types of individual life experiences. That said, this does not mean that the distinction between variation and diversity reduces to semantics. The mechanisms through which variation enhances robustness or, in the cases of systems with positive feedbacks, increases the likelihood of tips, differ from the mechanisms through which a diversity of types influences robustness. As I show in the next three chapters, diversity's impact takes many forms. Some, like its ability to provide insurance, are intuitive. Other effects, like its influence on innovation, are surprising.

6

DIVERSITY'S INESCAPABLE BENEFITS I: AVERAGING

> Science is nothing but trained and organized
> common sense.
> —Thomas H. Huxley

I now begin an analysis of the effects of diverse types on complex systems. I start with two (almost) inescapable benefits of diversity. These benefits go a long way toward explaining why scientifically minded people believe in the value of diversity. They explain why scientists and laypeople alike concerned with the preservation of ecosystems speak about the importance of species preservation. And why investment advisors talk about the importance of balanced portfolios.

These inescapable benefits result from two causes: averaging and diminishing returns to type. The first cause, averaging, refers to the fact that if you have lots of types, you've got some insurance. This prevents really bad outcomes from occurring. The second cause, diminishing returns to type, refers to the fact that in many contexts the marginal return (in productivity, profits, or fun) decreases the more you have of a type. Each additional piece of cake is a little less satisfying than the one that preceded it.

These two causes imply that diversity proves beneficial without any extra "magical" properties. What do I mean by that? I mean that diversity can produce benefits without the existence of any symbiotic or synergistic effects. It is these synergies—the chocolate plus hard candy shell that combine to produce M&Ms—that most people think of when explaining the benefits of diversity. Synergies like this do exist. The *E. coli* in our gut feed off us and at the same time help us to digest our food. Clearly, such synergies are great. But diversity produces benefits, large benefits, even without them.

In this chapter, I concentrate on the first cause of an inescapable benefit: averaging. I do this in three ways. First, I present the *Central Limit Theorem*, which formalizes how diverse types combine to reduce variation in performance. I extend this to the *Diversity Central Limit Theorem*, which relates reductions in variance to the *diversity index*. I then discuss portfolio theory from finance. This puts more structure on relationships between types and payoffs by including states of the world. I conclude with what I call the *Factor Limit Theorem*, which extends the logic of the central limit theorem and provides even deeper insights into the averaging effects of diversity. In the next chapter, I take up diminishing returns to type.

The core argument of this chapter goes as follows. Surviving requires a fitness or a payoff above some threshold. Diverse collections have greater attribute diversity. This diversity through averaging will prevent payoffs or fitness from falling below the threshold. In sum, simple averaging effects will imply that diverse systems are more robust (Doak et al. 1998). This effect will be more pronounced in complex systems because they produce so much fluctuation. The complete argument is a little more complicated in that the relevant diversity may be attribute diversity and not the number of types.

The Central Limit Theorem

A core lesson from statistics is that with independent disturbances, variation cancels out as the sample sizes grow larger. The daily earnings of, say, a cab driver show substantial fluctuations. Weekly earnings show less. Monthly earnings vary only a little. The same holds for the stock market, though the temporal scales differ. Daily index fund values float up and down drastically. Monthly and annual averages do not vary as much, and decade averages look relatively smooth (usually). The fact that variation cancels with larger sample sizes is no mere stylized fact. It is one of the most important theorems in mathematics: *the Central Limit Theorem*. Stated informally, this theorem states that with enough data, the mean of a sample equals the true mean: *variations cancel.* That cancellation enhances robustness.

The central limit theorem refers to an entire family of limit theorems. I present the most basic version. The theorem relies on the notion of *random variables*. These random variables take on a range of possible values. For example, the heights or weights of a collection of people will not all be the same. Instead, there is a *distribution*, and that distribution has a *mean* (an average value) and a *standard deviation*. The central limit theorem considers the average of a collection of random variables. It makes two assumptions. First, the random variables have to be *independent*. This means that the value of one random variable cannot be correlated with the value of another. Independence is a strong assumption and often doesn't hold. Nevertheless, independence proves a valuable benchmark, a modeling assumption that strips away details and helps identify main effects. The second assumption is more technical in nature. It requires that the random variables have finite standard deviations.

For random variables like my weight or the temperature in Bethesda, this assumption is easily satisfied. However, power law distributions, which arise frequently in complex systems, can have infinite standard deviation. In a power law distribution, the probability that a variable exceeds a value x is proportional to $x^{-\alpha}$. When α is larger than one, the variable need not even have a mean that is finite, let alone a finite standard deviation. The central limit theorem rules out these sorts of distributions.

The Central Limit Theorem

Let $X_1, X_2, \ldots, X_N$ be *independent* random variables. Assume that each has mean value μ and a standard deviation σ. Let $\bar{X}$ equal the average of the X_i variables,

$$\bar{X} = \frac{\sum_{i=1}^{N} X_i}{N}.$$

Central Limit Theorem: *The random variable $\bar{X}$ has mean μ and standard deviation $\frac{\sigma}{\sqrt{N}}$.*

Rather than apply the central limit theorem to the heights or weights of people, here I apply it to a collective measure, say, productivity. Imagine you have a garden with N types of plants. Each plant has a yield. The variable X_1 might denote the yield in pounds of tomatoes, and X_2 might denote the yield of string beans. For convenience, assume that you planted your garden so that the expected yield from each crop is the same. In other words, you expect to get the same number of pounds of beans as tomatoes.

The central limit theorem says that the standard deviation in your total yield falls by a factor equal to the square root of the number of crops, N. If each crop has a mean, μ, equal to 100 pounds and a standard deviation, σ, equal to 10, and if each crop's yield satisfies a normal distribution (it comes from a standard bell curve), then 95 percent of the time the yield of each crop will lie within two standard deviations of the mean—between 80 lbs and 120 lbs. The Central Limit Theorem tells us that with sixteen crops ($N = 16$), the average yield for all crops will have a standard deviation one fourth of that ($4 = \sqrt{16}$), which means that 95 percent of the time the average yield per crop will lie between 95 lb and 105 lb. Thus, diversity reduces variation. If to stay in business, a farmer must have a yield of, say, 90 lbs, the diverse planting will almost guarantee it.

This standard version of the central limit theorem considers the average of the N random variables. A generalization of the theorem allows for the variables to be assigned weights. This complicates the algebra, but not much. In fact, if we add weights, we can relate the standard deviation of the weighted average of the variables to the *diversity index*.

The Diversity Central Limit Theorem

Let $X_1, X_2, \ldots, X_N$ be *independent* random variables. Assume that each has mean value μ and standard deviation σ. Given a probability distribution $(p_1, p_2, \ldots, p_N)$ over the N variables, let $\bar{X}(p)$ equal the probability weighted average of the X_is:

$$\bar{X}(p) = \sum_{i=1}^{N} p_i X_i.$$

Diversity Central Limit Theorem: *The random variable $\bar{X}(p)$ has mean μ and standard deviation*
$$\frac{\sigma}{\sqrt{(\sum_{i=1}^{N} p_i^2)^{-1}}}.$$

The diversity central limit theorem is important for two reasons. First, it tells us that diversity, as measured by the diversity index, reduces variation in performance. Absent interactions between species in an ecosystem, if we were to do empirical tests on diversity and ecosystem robustness, we would find that more diverse ecosystems are more robust (Doak et al. 1998; Lhomme and Winkel 2002). This same logic holds for corporations that are conglomerates. Owning firms in more industries should make a conglomerate more robust to market fluctuations (Prahalad and Bettis 1986). Second, the theorem implies that if we have sufficient diversity, variation in performance can be driven almost to zero.

If the assumptions of the theorem hold true, we should expect diverse ecologies to have less variation in their rates of converting solar energy into biomass, we should expect diverse stock portfolios to have less variation in their returns, and we should expect large groups of forecasters to make accurate predictions. In broad strokes, these empirical predictions hold true. Yet, I am not quite able to place the "do not erase" sign on the chalkboard and move on to the next topic. The reason is that the diversity central limit theorem tells us more than just that variance should fall with diversity. It also tells us how fast it should fall—by a factor proportional to the diversity index. Here, the empirical evidence doesn't look so compelling. Diversity doesn't always reduce variation at the rate predicted by the theorem.

This does not mean that the theorem is incorrect. It means that one or more of the assumptions in the theorem don't hold when taken to the real world. The guilty party? The *independence assumption*. The independence assumption, if it held, would imply that species' fitnesses are not related, nor are the performances of stocks or the forecasts of meteorologists. Of course, none of this is true. Species fitnesses are inter-related, sometimes negatively and sometimes positively. Financial assets also have correlated values. Sometimes they go up and down together (oil stocks and airline stocks) and sometimes they go in opposite directions (oil stocks and green energy futures).

Also, keep in mind that interdependencies between the parts are a defining feature of complex systems. The independence assumption flies in the fact of interdependencies. To relax the independence assumption, I need more structure. I do that by introducing the concept of a *state space*. This enables me to tie performance to particular states of the world. I do this in the context of portfolio theory.

Portfolio Theory

Portfolio theory was developed to show how diversification spreads risk. In a portfolio model, an investor selects investments. These investments generate payoffs that depend in some way on the current condition of markets, industries, and economies, the so-called *state of the world.* To make this formal, I assume a finite number of states of the world. Given the state of the world, it is possible to predict the payoff of each investment. These investments need not be financial paper. And the payoffs need not be in dollars. The investments could represent crops (Di Falco and Perrings 2003) or energy sources. In the latter case, payoffs might be more aligned with security than gross domestic product.

What follows relies on definitions that appear a bit technical at first, but the logic is straightforward. First, I define the states of the world as follows:

The set of **states of the world** $\Omega = \{1, 2, \ldots, \omega\}$.

An investment, which can be thought of as a stock, has a payoff associated with each possible state of the world. The stock may have the same payoff in some states. That doesn't matter. What's relevant is that we can characterize an investment as a vector of payoffs, one for each state of the world.

An **investment** $\pi = (\pi_1, \pi_2, \ldots, \pi_\omega)$, *where each* π *is a real number.*

An example helps to clarify these first two definitions.

Example: The state of the world corresponds to the weather, which can be sunny, rainy, or overcast. Investing in an umbrella (*UM*) generates a payoff of one if it is sunny, twenty if it is rainy, and nothing if it is overcast. I can therefore characterize the umbrella as a vector of length three: $UM = (1, 20, 0)$.

To complete the model, I need probability assessments over the states of the world. Let p_i denote the probability of state i occurring. Each p_i must be at least zero and less than or equal to one.

*A **probability vector** over states* $p = (p_1, p_2, \ldots, p_\omega)$, *where* $p_i \geq 0$ *for all i and* $\sum_{i=1}^{\omega} p_i = 1$.

Given a probability vector, each investment has an *expected value*, which equals the average amount that the investment will pay.

*The **expected value** of investment s given the probability vector over states p equals*

$$E[s \mid p] = \sum_{i=1}^{\omega} p_i \cdot \pi_i.$$

Extending the earlier example, if sun, rain, and overcast weather are equally likely, then the probability of each state equals one third. This can be written formally as $p = (\frac{1}{3}, \frac{1}{3}, \frac{1}{3})$. It follows that the expected value of owning an umbrella equals seven:

$$E[UM \mid p] = \frac{1}{3} + \frac{20}{3} + \frac{0}{3} = 7.$$

To show the value of diversity requires more investments. Let's add sunglasses and a book. Their payoffs and associated expected values given the probability distribution p are as follows:

Sunglasses (SG): SG $= (18, 0, 0)$

$$E[SG \mid p] = \frac{18}{3} + \frac{0}{3} + \frac{0}{3} = 6.$$

Book (BK): BK $= (0, 9, 9)$

$$E[BK \mid p] = \frac{0}{3} + \frac{9}{3} + \frac{9}{3} = 6.$$

UM has the highest expected value of the three investments, so at first glance it seems like the best investment. However, two-thirds of the time, it generates a payoff of one or less. A risk averse investor would not be happy with no return, so the umbrella alone is not a very appealing investment. This point, that it is not expected payoff that matters, is crucial to thinking about diversity and robustness. If this were an ecosystem or a political system, a payoff of zero might correspond to total collapse. One admittedly crude way to think about robustness is to think of maintenance of a performance level above some threshold. As we shall see, greater diversity increases this probability.

To avoid overcomplicating the model, assume that each investment costs $5, and we have $15 dollars to spend. How should the investor allocate her money across these investments? Consider the following three portfolios:

UM Portfolio $UM = 2, SG = 0, BK = 0.$

One–Two Portfolio $UM = 0, SG = 1, BK = 2.$

All Three Portfolio $UM = 1, SG = 1, BK = 1.$

The *UM* portfolio's payoff vector equals three times the payoff vector of the *UM* investment, or $(3, 60, 0)$. The One–Two portfolio' payoff vector equals the sum of the *SG* investment's payoff vector $(18, 0, 0)$ and two times the *BK* investment's payoff vector $(0, 18, 18)$, which is $(18, 18, 18)$. Finally, the All Three portfolio has a payoff vector that equals the sum of the three investment's individual payoff vectors: $(19, 29, 9)$.

There are several ways to evaluate these portfolios. I have already discussed the notion of *expected value*, which is how much the portfolio pays on average. We can also look at the worst payoff and the median payoff. In the table below, I compute each of these measures for all three of the portfolios.

Portfolio	Payoff Vector	Expected Value	Worst Case Scenario	Median Payoff
UM	$(3, 60, 0)$	21	0	3
One–Two	$(18, 18, 18)$	18	18	18
All Three	$(19, 29, 9)$	19	9	19

When looking at the portfolios in this way, the One–Two portfolio stands out as the best choice for someone risk averse even though it has the lowest expected value. The One–Two portfolio offers perfect insurance. No matter what the state of the world, the payoff will always be eighteen dollars. The other two portfolios fare poorly on overcast days. The *UM* portfolio pays nothing and the All Three portfolio pays out only nine dollars.

This example helps us to think about diversity differently. If we think of diversity at the level of investments, then the All Three portfolio is the most diverse, as it is the only portfolio that contains all three investments. However, if we interpret diversity at the level of payoffs in the possible states of the world, the One–Two portfolio is the most diverse.

The Factor Limit Theorem

The portfolio model assumes payoffs are a function of the state of the world. The stocks in an actual portfolio exhibit correlation owing to the fact that they are influenced by common *factors*, such as the health of the overall economy, oil prices, consumer confidence, political events, and so on. The same is true in ecosystems. Species exhibit correlations in success based on common *functionalities* and *attributes*. If entities, be they species or stock, contain overlapping attributes, then their payoffs will be correlated and this will limit the amount of independence that can be produced.

The idea that the success of individual entities (be they stocks or species) depends on common factors can be made explicit by writing the value of an entity as a function of these factors as well as of other entity-specific random variables. For instance, the value of a real estate company owning properties in Hawaii might depend on a common factor that influences many stocks, such as the price of oil, as well as on company-specific random variables, such as the level of rainfall in Hawaii available, which would have no effect on the stock price of Google. Similarly, the yield from a tomato plant might depend on common factors that influence other plants, like sunlight and rainfall, as well as plant-specific factors, such as the number of aphids on the plant.

The model I now describe is a variant of the *Asset Pricing Model* (Sharpe 1964). In that model, there exist M

system-wide factors denoted by F_1 through F_M and N times M entities. Each of the factors influences the values of the NM distinct entities, which are denoted by Y_{ij}.[53] (The notation's a little cumbersome.) In the model, the value of the entity Y_{ij} depends on the ith factor, F_i, and on the value of an entity-specific random variable, denoted by X_{ij}. To complete the model, the variable β captures the relative weight of the system-wide factor:

$$Y_{ij} = \beta F_i + (1 - \beta) X_{ij}$$

If β equals zero, the values of the entities are independent. If β equals one, it's as if there are only M entities, one for each factor. Keep in mind that the factors are random variables. Owing to the fact that the values of the individual entities depend on the factors, the sum of all the values depends on the variation in these factors. And given that the variation due to the factors remains fixed, even if we have a large number of entities influenced by each factor (a large N), variation can never go away entirely. That intuition can be made formal in what I call the *Factor Limit Theorem*.

The Factor Limit Theorem

Let $F_1, F_2, \ldots, F_M$ be random variables designated as *factors* that are independent with mean ν and standard deviation γ. Let $X_{11}, X_{12}, \ldots, X_{1N}, \ldots, X_{M1}, X_{M2}, \ldots, X_{MN}$ be *independent* random variables. Assume that each has mean value μ and standard deviation σ.

Let $Y_{ij} = \beta F_i + (1-\beta) X_{ij}$ be random variables each of whose value depends on a single factor as well as an independent random variable. Let $\bar{Y}$ equal the average of the Y_{ij} variables.

$$\bar{Y} = \frac{\sum_{i=1}^{M} \sum_{j=1}^{N} Y_{ij}}{MN}$$

Factor Limit Theorem: *The random variable $\bar{Y}$ has mean $\beta v + (1 - \beta)\mu$ and standard deviation $\frac{\beta \gamma}{\sqrt{M}} + \frac{(1-\beta)\sigma}{\sqrt{MN}}$. In the special case $\gamma = \sigma$, the standard deviation equals $\frac{\sqrt{N}\beta\sigma + (1-\beta)}{\sqrt{MN}}$.*

The factor limit theorem shows that the variation in the average value depends on two terms—the variation in the factors $\frac{\beta \gamma}{\sqrt{M}}$ and the variation in the entity specific random variables. Only the second term depends on N. Thus, increasing the number of types of entities can only reduce variation to the extent those entities are influenced by new factors. In other words, I could not reduce the variation in a stock portfolio by investing in more companies if those new companies' values were influenced by common factors. There's a limit to how much variation that can exist. That limit is determined by the diversity of attributes as I discuss in the summary.

Summary

In this chapter I have shown how averaging implies a benefit to diversity. Systems with more types will be more robust because they are less likely to have bad outcomes. That insight was formalized with three different theorems: the central limit theorem, the diversity central limit theorem, and the factor limit theorem. These theorems all imply that diversification reduces performance variation and therefore contributes to robustness.

The fact that diversification reduces variation increases survivability, but it does not mean that diverse approaches will be the top performers. To the contrary, the best portfolios in any given year won't be diverse. On many college campuses, a firm or club will sponsor an investment competition. The team that wins typically does not invest in a diversified portfolio. Nor do the teams that do worst. The diversified portfolios tend to be near the center. That's exactly what the theorems tell us to expect.

Two points mentioned during the chapter merit expanding. First, the theorems shed light on the different ways diversity reduces variation in outcomes. The central limit theorem implies that if payoffs are independent, then more types result in lower variance. The diversity central limit theorem implies that any reallocation across types that increases the diversity index will reduce variation provided that all types have the same expected value. Finally, the factor limit theorem implied that it's not just the number of types or their distribution, but the factors that influence them, and that greater diversity in the number of influencing factors will lead to less performance variation.

Second, notice how these insights correspond to our measures of diversity. The central limit theorem relies on number of types and the diversity central limit theorem relates variation to the diversity index. Finally, the factor limit theorem implicitly ties variation to attribute measures of diversity. Entities, be they stocks or species, that have similar attributes are likely to be influenced by similar factors. An ecosystem may have many species and a portfolio may consist of many stocks, but if the performance of those species (resp. stocks) depends on a single factor, the system may well be volatile.

To come full circle, it's true that averaging implies an inescapable benefit to diversity, but only if we're careful about how we define diversity. If the system consists of no interactions, diversity can be captured by the number of types or by the diversity index. More types will mean less performance variation. But if the performance of a system depends on the functions that entities perform, then a simple number of types or diversity index won't suffice to explain system performance. An attribute-based measure will be required. Maintaining robust ecosystem may requiring preserving the maximal number of functions—such as the ability to decompose leaves on the forest floor—which might be at odds with maximizing the number of species.

In a complex system, the factors can often be other entities. The fitness of the bee depends on the prevalence of flower blossoms, and the value of a rubber company depends on the health of the auto industry. That said, regardless of what the factors are, diverse systems should perform better because of the effect of averaging across all the factors. That's one reason why diversity's benefits are often inescapable. In the next chapter, I show how diminishing returns to type provide a second reason.

7

DIVERSITY'S INESCAPABLE BENEFITS II: DIMINISHING RETURNS TO TYPES

> Knowledge is the only instrument of production that is
> not subject to diminishing returns.
> —JOHN MAURICE CLARKE

In this chapter, I show how diminishing returns to type provide a second inescapable benefit of diversity. When diminishing returns to type are present, diverse collections do best. Suppose we had an empirical question as to whether diversity improves performance in some context. We may want to understand whether racial or gender diversity improves group problem solving efficiency, whether species diversity enhances ecological robustness, or whether economic diversity increases productivity. As long as diminishing returns are present, we'll usually find a benefit to diversity.

Diminishing returns to type exist if the contribution to some performance measure such as efficiency, robustness, or accuracy decreases with the amount of a type. This does not mean that the output falls. It only means that output rises at a diminishing rate. Diminishing returns are a widespread phenomenon in economies and ecosystems. Additional workers of the same type contribute diminishing returns to the total product. Economists call this the *diminishing marginal product of labor*. And, in most cases, the effect of adding more members of a species to an ecosystem will also satisfy diminishing returns to productivity. Ecologists refer to this as *frequency-dependent fitness*. Even if two species have a symbiotic interaction, the effect of that interaction will typically diminish as one species becomes more prevalent for the simple reason that it has fewer of the other species with whom to interact.

To show how diminishing returns within type produces a benefit of diversity, I construct simple models of ecosystem survivability. These models build from a thought experiment about whether ecosystem diversity improves robustness. Imagine that I drive to a Wal-Mart and purchase twenty or so plastic kiddie pools and then go to a nursery and buy several species of water plants. In some pools, I place a single species of plant. In other pools, I include two or three species. And, finally, in a few pools, I place every species. I could then classify the three types of pools as homogeneous, moderately diverse, and highly diverse. At the end of the summer, I could return to see which of the ecosystems survived. If on average, the species' contributions to survivability exhibit diminishing returns, then the diverse samples will be more likely to survive. This will be true even if there is no direct benefit from diversity—no real synergies.

Using this thought experiment of ecosystems of different levels of diversity as a framework, I construct four examples. In the first three examples, diversity plays no direct role: the contribution of any one species to the ecosystem's survivability does not depend on the other species. It depends only on the number of its own species in the system. In the last example, I assume that diversity actually lowers survivability of the system. In other words, I assume a negative interaction between diverse types. And yet, even here I show that diversity appears to have a positive empirical effect. I then state what I call the *Diminishing Returns Diversity Theorem*. I end with a small caveat and a final comment on how even when diversity doesn't produce any direct benefits, it may still be beneficial.

Four Examples and the Diminishing Returns Diversity Theorem

I now present four examples in which I compare the robustness of orchards under different circumstances. In the first example, the effect of diversity will appear similar to an averaging effect, but in the other examples, it will become clear that the diminishing returns effect is of a different type. In these examples, the orchards contain diverse types of fruit trees: apple (denoted by A), banana (B), cherry (C), and date (D).[54] I'll refer to an orchard with three trees as an *ecosystem*. A little math shows that there are twenty possible ecosystems. These can be classified as *diverse*, *moderate*, and *homogeneous*.

Diverse: *ecosystems that contain three types of trees.*

ABC	ABD	ACD	BCD

Moderate: *ecosystems that contain two types of trees.*

ABB	AAB	AAC	ACC
AAD	ADD	BBC	BCC
BBD	BDD	CCD	CDD

Homogeneous: *ecosystems that contain one type of tree.*

$$\boxed{\text{AAA} \quad \text{BBB} \quad \text{CCC} \quad \text{DDD}}$$

In each of the examples that follow, I compare the average probabilities of survival of each of the three classes of ecosystems.

Example #1: An Apple a Day Keeps the Doctor Away

In this first example, any ecosystem with an apple tree survives with certainty, and any ecosystem without an apple tree dies with certainty. To calculate the average robustness level for each class, I need only calculate the percentage of ecosystems within each class that contain an apple tree. Of the four diverse ecosystems, three contain an apple tree, so the average probability of survival is 75 percent. Six of the twelve moderate ecosystems contain an apple tree, so they have an average probability of survival of 50 percent. But, only one of the four homogeneous ecosystems contains an apple tree. Therefore, they have an average probability of survival of only 25 percent.

Average Probabilities of Survival: Example #1

Ecosystem Classification	Average Prob(Survive)
Diverse	75%
Moderate	50%
Homogeneous	25%

As the table shows, the diverse ecosystems have the highest average probability of survival. Yet, diversity per se does not drive survivability. Apple trees do. Diversity proves beneficial because more diverse ecosystems are more likely to contain apple trees, the single robust species.

Example #2: More Apples Up on Top

In the second example, survivability again only depends on apple trees, but in this example the more apple trees, the more likely the ecosystem survives. In addition, the benefits of additional apple trees decrease with the number of apple trees: the first apple tree increases survivability more than the second, and the second more than the third. In this example, I set the probability of survival for an ecosystem with one, two, and three apples tree to 60, 90, and 100 percent, respectively. These numerical values capture my three core assumptions: only apple trees matter, more apple trees are better, and the added benefit of an additional apple tree decreases with the number of apple trees.

Among the four diverse ecosystems, three contain exactly one apple tree. Each of those three ecosystems has a probability of survival of 60 percent and the fourth, BCD, which contains no apple tree, has a probability of survival of zero. Therefore, the average probability of survival is 45 percent $(45 = \frac{(3*60+1*0)}{4})$. Of the twelve moderate ecosystems, exactly half contain apple trees. Three contain two apple trees and three contain only one apple tree. A straightforward calculation gives an average probability of survival of 37.5 percent. Finally, only a single homogeneous ecosystem contains an apple tree, and it has three, so its probability of survival is 100 percent. Therefore, the average across all four homogeneous ecosystems is 25 percent.

Once again, on average the diverse ecosystems perform best. This result obtains even though diverse ecosystems do

Average Probabilities of Survival: Example #2

Ecosystem Classification	Average Prob(Survive)
Diverse	45%
Moderate	37.5%
Homogeneous	25%

not, on average, have more apple trees. And, as before, the diverse ecosystems are more likely to contain at least one apple tree. Recall that the first apple tree contributes more to performance than the either the second or the third. It is not only averaging that is driving the benefit to diversity. Diminishing returns do as well. How they do becomes clearer in the next example.

Example #3: Diminishing Contributions

Up to this point, only apple trees have contributed to survivability. In this third example, I make two assumptions. First, all four types of trees contribute to survivability, and second, as in Example #2, the contribution of additional trees of the same type decreases with the number of trees of that type. For each type of tree, I assume a different contribution to survivability for each additional tree. These assumed contributions can be written in a *Survivability Contribution Table*.

Survivability Contribution Table: Example #3

Tree Type	Tree #1	Tree #2	Tree #3
Apple	50	20	10
Banana	30	20	10
Cherry	20	20	10
Date	20	10	10

This table can be read as follows: the first banana tree contributes 30 to survivability, the second 20. To calculate the probability of survival of the ecosystem *BBD*, these two contributions are added to the contribution of the single date tree (20), which gives a total of 70 (70 = 30 + 20 + 20). Using the same logic, the ecosystem *AAA* has a probability of survival of 80, and the ecosystems *ABC* and *ABD* have a 100 percent probability of survival.

Calculating the average probabilities of survival for each of the three classes of ecosystems involves some algebra. Consider the four diverse ecosystems *ABC*, *ABD*, *ACD*, and *BCD*. Calculating their probabilities of survival requires adding three numbers from the first column of the contributions table. Calculating the probability of survival for each of the four homogeneous ecosystems requires adding across the columns in the contribution table. Given the assumption of diminishing contributions, the numbers in the first column are at least as large as the numbers in the second column, which are at least as large as those in the third column. Given that the average values in columns two and three are less than the average values in column one, the diverse ecosystems must be more likely to survive than the homogeneous ecosystems.

What about the moderate ecosystems? Calculating the probability of survival of *BBC* entails taking two numbers from the first column of the contribution table (for the first banana tree and the single cherry tree) and one number from the second column. This same pattern holds when computing the probability of survival for any moderate ecosystem. The final value will be the sum of two values from the first column and one from the second. A moment's reflection reveals that the moderate ecosystems must be less likely to survive than the diverse ecosystems, which only take numbers from the first column, but more likely to survive than the homogenous ecosystems, which take numbers from all three columns.

Explicit calculations give the following average survivability values. More important than the actual numbers though is the intuition that diverse ecosystems draw values from the first column and the other ecosystems draw values from the other columns as well. And those other columns have lower values due to diminishing returns to type.

Average Probabilities of Survival: Example #3

Ecosystem Classification	Average Prob(Survive)
Diverse	90%
Moderate	77.5%
Homogeneous	57.5%

Diminishing Returns and the Benefits of Diversity

I now show that these three examples all fit within a general class of performance functions and, for any example within that class, diversity improves performance. Performance need not be survivability of an ecosystem. It could be productivity of an economy, or it could be number of patents introduced by a research laboratory. To state that theorem, I need to make two assumptions.

Diminishing Returns (DR): *The contribution to performance of an additional entity of a type strictly decreases with the number of at least one type and does not increase for any of the other types.*

Absence of Interactions (AI): *Total performance equals the sum of the contributions across the types.*

The first assumption implies that the values in the marginal contribution table do not increase along any row. This clearly holds in the third example, and a moment's reflection reveals that its true of the first two example as well. In those examples, for all but the apple trees, contributions equal zero. So the contribution to performance does not increase for those types of trees. For the apple trees, the contribution to performance strictly decreases. So, DR holds.

With any assumption, a natural question to ask is whether it holds in the real world. I focus first on DR. Suppose that we are considering groups of people solving a problem and that type represents field of training. The standard assumption from economics would be that the first engineer is more valuable to a group than the second, and the second is more valuable than the third. The same would be true for adding mathematicians to a research group. The first mathematician might be quite helpful, the tenth less so. In an ecosystem, each additional member of a species might similarly contribute less to ecosystem efficiency (as measured by energy transfer). At some point, that contribution might become negative. Note that the DR assumption does not preclude negative contributions.

Diminishing returns is also a standard assumption in utility theory. The first scoop of ice cream is assumed to bring more utility than the second, the second more than the third, and the third more than the fourth. Ice cream provides an extreme example, but the same effect is assumed to hold for automobiles, shirts, and ski chalets. More is better but increasingly less so.

The assumption that system level performance equals the sum of the types' performance is less realistic. In almost all interesting cases, interactions between diverse types influence performance. That's especially true in complex systems. Nevertheless, the assumption provides an important benchmark. In some cases, interaction effects will improve performance. In other cases, interaction effects will hinder performance. The theorem reveals a general bias toward diversity appearing beneficial.

The Diminishing Returns Diversity Theorem

Let $F(x_1, x_2, \ldots, x_N)$ equal the performance of N entities. Assume that each entity is one of T types. Assume that the performance function F satisfies DR and AI. If $K > M$, then the average performance of all sets of N entities with exactly K types exceeds the average performance of collections with exactly M types.

This theorem says that so long as the types satisfy diminishing returns and there are no interactions between the types, on average more diversity implies better performance. Complex systems contain myriad interactions between diverse types. Some improve outcomes. Some don't.[55] If those interactions are on average positive, then diverse collections will do even better, so there is no need to consider that case. Interactions, however, need not be beneficial. In social systems, they often create conflict. In the last example, I include costs to diversity and show that it can still be beneficial even when diminishing returns to type are present.

Example #4: Costs to Diversity

In this example, I assume that each pair of types produces a negative interaction term that hinders performance. Yet, diversity will still be beneficial. This example builds from example #3, only now, for each pair of distinct types present in an ecosystem, the probability the ecosystem survives drops by X percent. Diversity is harmful. For ease of presentation, I assume that the average probabilities for survival for the ecosystems are otherwise the same as in example #3.

Given the assumption of negative interactions between pairs of diverse types, the average probability of survival of the moderate ecosystems decreases by X percent because each moderate ecosystem contains one pair of distinct types. Similarly, each diverse ecosystem contains three distinct pairs of species (AB, AC, and BC), so its probability of survival decreases by $3X$ percent. Borrowing from example #3, the probabilities of survival can be written as follows:

Average Probabilities of Survival: Example #4

Ecosystem Classification	Average Prob(Survive)
Diverse	$(90 - 3X)\%$
Moderate	$(77.5 - X)\%$
Homogeneous	57.5%

A quick calculation shows that if X is less than 6.25 percent, the diverse ecosystems will still be most robust. A similar calculation shows that for the homogeneous ecosystems to be more likely to survive than the diverse ones, the variable X

has to be almost 11 percent. This example drives home the general point: *even with substantial negative interaction effects, diminishing returns will imply that diverse collections perform better.*

A Caveat and a Surprising Conclusion

A quick review may be helpful at this point. We have seen that decreasing contributions from types imply that diverse collections perform best on average. This occurs without any explicit benefits to diversity, any so-called synergies. We have also seen that diverse collections can perform best on average even when diversity creates harmful interactions. Hence, the benefits to diversity are (almost) inescapable.

The results from this section do not imply that when confronted with a novel situation we should always choose a diverse collection. If we have enough information to know what drives performance, then we should select the best collection on the basis of that information. If not, and if we only get one try, then we should probably choose a diverse collection. This does not mean that diversity is always better, only that if we are not sure of what we're doing, we should err toward greater diversity.

Before interpreting these results further, a caveat is in order. In this chapter, I calculated average values, an unsophisticated statistical test that confounds the benefits from diversity and returns to scale. With sufficient data, I could construct a statistical test to determine the returns to scale and the explicit benefits (or costs) of diversity. Using proper statistics, I would, in the examples that I covered, find no explicit benefit to diversity. That's because I did not include any synergies. Does this imply that diversity doesn't improve performance? No. Quite the opposite. Diversity does improve performance and it does so without synergies! That's the main point of the previous chapter and this one: *averaging and diminishing returns to type generate a benefit to diversity.*

In both this and the previous chapter, I've taken most of the complexity out of the systems by not allowing interactions. I did so to make a more general point—in order for diversity not to be beneficial the interactions must be negative, as shown in example #4. These two simple causes, averaging and diminishing return, go a long way toward explaining why diversity is so important to complex systems. They show that as long as the interactions between diverse types don't produce exceptionally large negative interactive effects, then the average performance of diverse collections should perform better than that of more moderate or homogeneous collections.

Furthermore, given that complex systems often self-assemble through selection, we might expect a tendency toward more synergistic (positive) interactions than antagonistic ones. Therefore, we might expect diversity to be even more beneficial in complex systems than in noncomplex systems.

That's the topic I turn to next.

8

DIVERSITY'S IMPACT IN COMPLEX SYSTEMS

I do not know, as I have often said, a better school
wherein to model life than by incessantly exposing to it
the diversity of so many other lives, fancies, and usances,
and by making it relish a perpetual variety of forms of
human nature.
—MONTAIGNE, OF VANITY

In the previous two chapters I showed how diversity can improve system performance through averaging and diminishing returns to type. Those results assumed limited interactions between diverse types, and therefore few or no synergies. In this chapter, I describe the myriad ways in which diversity impacts complex systems when interactions are present.

I demonstrate how diversity enables systems to flourish, to be robust, and also touch on efficiency and innovativeness. Clearly, to be robust a system must have some level of efficiency and must be able to innovate in the face of change, so these effects will be related. My approach will be to focus on the mechanisms through which diversity operates. Unlike in the previous two chapters, here I will emphasize synergies.

I describe ten mechanisms that contribute to system robustness—the ability of the system to flourish. This list is by no means exhaustive, nor the only possible categorization, but it's a start.

- Specialization I: Comparative Advantage
- Specialization II: Learning by Doing
- Responsiveness
- Competition
- Synergies I: Superadditive Tricks
- Synergies II: Multiple Landscapes
- Synergies III: Diversity Production
- Collective Knowledge
- Redundancy and Degeneracy
- Firewalling and Modularity
- Cross Cutting Cleavages

Specialization I: Comparative Advantage

To first show how diversity can promote synergistic effects, I describe a static model of comparative advantage. The first known analysis of comparative advantage is due to Torrens (1815). For novelty's sake, I'll present it as a model of a partnership between two people: Aisha and Bob. Aisha and Bob each possess the ability to collect two products: fish and coconuts. Both Aisha and Bob's ideal is to consume equal amounts of each (measured by pounds). The table below displays their relative abilities at each task. Aisha can catch 160 lbs of fish or gather 240 lbs of coconuts per month. Bob, who's less capable than Aisha, can catch 20 lbs of fish or gather

80 lbs of coconuts.

Output per Month		
Person	Fish	Coconuts
Aisha	160	240
Bob	20	80

In the absence of trade, Bob and Aisha divide up their days so as to produce equal amounts of fish and coconuts. For convenience, I'll assume that a month has 30 days. Aisha will therefore spend eighteen days catching fish and twelve days gathering coconuts. Bob, meanwhile, will spend twenty-four days catching fish and six days gathering coconuts.[56]

No Trade

Aisha		
Product	Days	Output
Fish	18	**96**
Coconuts	12	**96**

Bob		
Product	Days	Output
Fish	24	**16**
Coconuts	6	**16**

Even though Bob is less productive at each task, both Bob and Aisha would benefit from trade. This benefit comes from the fact that Bob is four times as effective gathering coconuts as he is at catching fish, while Aisha is only 50 percent better. Or, to put the insight another way, Bob is so inept at catching fish, both benefit if he only gathers coconuts and trades for whatever fish he needs. This is the insight from the theory of *comparative advantage*: two people should trade if one has a relative advantage over the other in some mutually desired output.

To see the magnitude of the advantages of trade, suppose that Bob only gathers coconuts.

Bob		
Product	Days	Output
Fish	0	**0**
Coconuts	30	**80**

To balance out the total production of fish and coconuts, Aisha must spend more time catching fish than she did when there was no trade.

Aisha		
Product	Days	Output
Fish	24	**128**
Coconuts	6	**48**

I will ignore the price at which Bob and Aisha decide to trade fish for coconuts and focus only on the gains in total production. Prior to trade, total production of each good was 112 lb per month. After trade begins, total production increases to 128 lb per month, over a 14 percent increase.

We think of trade as a purely economic activity, but similar dynamics can occur within any complex system. Entities that generalize may find that they do better by specializing at those activities for which they have a relative advantage. Diversity, therefore, can produce increases in efficiency for the rather obvious reason that it allows entities to do what they do best.

Specialization II: Learning by Doing

The comparative advantage model above does not include learning. The next model demonstrates the increased benefits from specialization when the actors can learn. In this model, there are also two people, who following tradition, I call Robinson and Friday. They live on an island. Robinson and Friday also live on coconuts and fish. Robinson and Friday are both intelligent people. The more they do something, the better they perform. Business professors and psychologists call this improvement *learning by doing* (Arrow 1962). Every day, billions of people improve at their daily tasks. Some of this learning is attributable to learning to interpret problems or situations in a new way, and some results from new technologies.

Empirical evidence suggests that learning rates tend to decrease over time. A worker at a new job may get 10 percent better the first year, another 5 percent the second year, and only 1 percent the third year. This has nothing to do with a decrease in effort. It has everything to do with the fact that the easy improvements are found first and that, over time, improving becomes more difficult.

I assume that Robinson and Friday want to eat as much fish and as many coconuts as possible and that each wants to work exactly ten hours per day. If each can pick one coconut per hour or catch one fish per hour, then their total production equals ten coconuts and ten fish. It does not matter how they allocate their time between fishing and picking coconuts so long as they jointly spend equal amounts of time at each task.

In what follows, I assume a learning rate of 24 percent divided by the number of years spent exclusively at that task. If Robinson only picks coconuts, he'll improve at 24 percent the first year, 12 percent the second year, 6 percent the third year, and so on. If he picks coconuts half of the time and catches fish half of the time, then he'll improve at half that rate: 12 percent the first year at both tasks, 6 percent the second year, and so on. However, he'll get better at both tasks, not just one. The same analysis holds for Friday. The table below shows Robinson's (or Friday's) learning rates with and without specialization over the next ten years.

Learning Rates with and without Specialization

Year	1	2	3	4	5	6	7	8	9	10
Without Specialization	12	12	6	6	4	4	3	3	2.4	2.4
With Specialization	24	12	8	6	4.8	4	3.43	3	2.66	2.4

The graph below shows per capita productivity beginning in year 1, both with and without specialization and continuing through the next ten years. With specialization, productivity grows over 94 percent; but without specialization, productivity grows by less than 70 percent. In the box below, I extend this example to a more general case where there are N tasks and N individuals and a learning rate of r/t, where t denotes the number of periods working at the task.

Specialization and Productivity

Assume N individuals and N tasks. Let time be indexed as discrete periods $t = 1, 2, \ldots$. Assume that productivity per task equals one initially and improves by r/t percent for each full period spent at a task. Let $T = kN$. If each individual is a **generalist** and performs all N tasks, then after T periods, per capita productivity equals:

$$\left(\Pi_{t=1}^{k} \left(1 + \frac{r}{tN} \right) \right)^{N}$$

If each individual **specializes**, then per capita productivity equals:

$$\Pi_{t=1}^{T} \left(1 + \frac{r}{t} \right)$$

It's straightforward to show that for $r > 0$, the second ratio exceeds the first and the limit of the ratios approaches infinity as the number of tasks, N, goes to infinity.

The result in the box implies that as the task becomes further and further decomposed, the relative advantage of specialization increases to infinity.[57] This shows how specialization creates an advantage within a complex system: If entities continue to improve over time at their tasks, then having fewer tasks increases the rate of improvement.[58]

Responsiveness

I next consider how diversity effects responsiveness, the ability of the system to respond to disturbances. That disturbance could be some new action. It could be a shift in a variable, such as temperature, or it could be the entry of a new species,

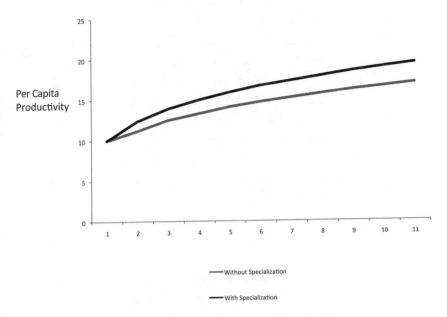

Figure 8.1. Increase in productivity due to specialization.

product, or idea—a Coke bottle might fall from the sky. Regardless of the nature of the change, stabilization of a system requires an opposing reaction lest the Coke bottle send the society spiraling off on a different path.

Responsiveness contributes to robustness—to be robust a system must be able to respond. In standard usage, responsiveness refers to the capacity to take a single action to cancel out the effects of some change. Robustness allows for adaptations that increase capacities and set a system on a new path. Thus, here, in considering responsiveness, I'm limiting my attention to actions that counteract changes.

Some context helps. Newton's Third Law states that for every action there must exist an equal and opposite reaction. A bird flapping its wings pushes air downward and as a result flies upward. Newton's law holds for closed systems.

Social, biological, and intellectual systems are open. In an open system, no such law need hold: an action need not have an opposite reaction. True, constraints on budgets, biomass, and cognitive attention do exist, placing some push back on actions. But, the lack of a necessary *countervailing action* makes maintaining functionality more of a challenge. In this section, I show that the greater the diversity of possible responses, the more disturbances a system can absorb. For each type of disturbance, the system must contain some counteracting response.

An Immune System Model

To demonstrate the logic of how diversity creates responsiveness, I construct a crude model of an immune system to show diverse responsiveness in action. Immune systems can be categorized as either *innate* or *adaptive*. An innate immune system has a fixed set of responses involving killer cells, phagocytes, and the like. These exist in fixed amounts. Think of the pathogen as a mold spreading on a windowpane. The innate immune system works like a child with a bottle of Windex and some Formula 409. When the pathogen arrives, the innate immune system comes out firing with both bottles. Maybe both work. Maybe one does. Sometimes neither does.

An adaptive immune system differs in three ways. First, it responds to the pathogen or antigen by building a specific solution. Think of a little chemistry lab in your body with miniature chemists mixing up concoctions to eradicate viruses. Second, its response has a lag. When our internal chemistry lab finds a solution that works, it starts making bigger and bigger batches of it. Third, an adaptive immune system maintains a memory of the attacker so that any new invasion will be tackled immediately. So, once our internal chemistry lab has made carpet stain remover, we can call it up whenever we need it.

Vaccination exploits this systemic memory. Though I want to avoid normative statements, clearly an adaptive immune system is preferable. In the United States chestnut trees, elm trees, and recently ash trees have been all but wiped out by single attackers because the trees' bottles of Windex weren't up to the task.

So why don't trees have adaptive immune systems? Well, they're costly. Think how much a bottle of Windex costs and compare that against even a modest chemistry lab. The real question may be: why would any species incur the cost of an adaptive immune system? The answer may hearken back to the old "red in tooth and claw" image. So far, adaptive immune systems have only been identified in species that have jaws. Some speculate that having a jaw makes a species more likely to fight and, as a result, more likely to be injured or infected (Matsunaga and Rahman 1998).

To see how diversity improves responsiveness, I describe a toy model of an immune system first described by Epstein and Axtell (1996). Though crude, the model can accommodate features of both types of immune systems. In the first version, the model does not manufacture solutions. It's akin to an innate immune system. When a pathogen attacks, either a solution exists in the library or it does not. If a solution exists, the entity lives. If a solution doesn't, the entity dies. In the second version, the immune system will be able to evolve responses, though not with anything near the sophistication of a real immune system. Nevertheless, the model proves instructive.

In the model, a virus is written as a list of 0s and 1s, and an immune system as a longer list of 0s and 1s. An immune system eradicates a virus if and only if a sublist of the immune system matches the virus perfectly. The example below shows a virus of length three and three immune systems of length eight. Notice that the first and third immune systems can eradicate the virus, but the second cannot:

Virus *010*

Immune System S1: *000<u>10</u>101*

Immune System S2: *11111110*

Immune System S3: *1<u>1010</u>0011*

Even though the three immune systems each have the same length, they differ in their ability to eradicate viruses. For each immune system, define its *immunity diversity* (ID) to be the number of unique viruses of length three that it can recognize and kill:

ID(S1) = **4** {000, 001, 010, 101}

ID(S2) = **2** {111, 110}

ID(S3) = **6** {101, 010, 100, 000, 001, 011}

Notice that immune system S3 *dominates* immune system S1. All four viruses eradicated by S1 are also eradicated by S3. Note also that immune system S3 offers maximal immunity: an immune system of length eight can eradicate at most six of the eight possible viruses of length three. This implies that such an immune system can produce a 75 percent chance of survival from a randomly selected virus.

Notice also that even though no individual can survive every virus attack, a diverse community can. Given any virus, either S2 or S3 can fight it off. The ability to fight off a single virus does not imply immunity to multiple viruses. For example, a community of S2s and S3s could not survive the virus 111 followed by the virus 000. For this reason, just counting the number of types of viruses that at least one member of the population can eradicate is not a good measure of community diversity, nor is any generalized entropy measure that counts the members of the population that can eradicate each virus. We need to use a more sophisticated measure that depends on attributes.

I now extend this model to make immunity adaptive. To do this, I assume the immune systems of offspring are combinations of the immune systems of their parents. Recall the elaboration of a genetic algorithm and how it produces new strings through inversion, recombination, and mutation. If we apply a genetic algorithm to this immune system model, we find that if we begin with diverse immune systems, then the genetic algorithm maintains diversity.

In the adaptive context, the appropriate measure of immunity diversity considers the entire community. The strings of length eight allow 256 unique immune systems. Computing the entropy over these 256 types would be one possible measure of a community's immunity, but this measure would treat the immune systems S1, S2, and S3 equally, even though they differ in how many viruses they can eradicate. Therefore, a better approach is to use an attribute-based diversity measure, where the attributes correspond to an ability to eradicate specific viruses.

The model shows the importance of immunity diversity. Immunity levels have played a large role in human history. In *Guns, Germs, and Steel,* Jared Diamond makes the argument that prolonged exposure to livestock meant that the Europeans had more advanced immune systems than Native Americans (Diamond 1999). This, he argues, is why a large percentage of Native Americans were wiped out by disease soon after the explorers and settlers arrived. I want to reconstruct his argument using the toy model of immunity described above.

To do this, I construct a simple thought experiment. Suppose that one society has been exposed to lots of viruses and that another has not. The most robust ecologies of immune systems will be diverse. Moreover, the most robust individuals will also have diverse immune systems, in the sense that they can combat the most viruses.

Assume that two societies suddenly mix and that each carries with it some viruses. I will assume that the first society brings more viruses than the second. To complete the thought experiment, I need to make some assumptions about the diversity of the immune systems within and across the members of each society. Here, I will consider viruses of length five so that I have greater potential diversity. I will assume that of the thirty-two possible viruses of length five, each member of the first society's immune system can kill fourteen of them. I will also assume that the immune systems of members of the second society can only kill twelve.

As for the diversity levels across people, I will assume that the members of the first society share four common substrings of length five and randomly differ on the other ten, while members of the second society share eight common substrings and differ on the other four that they can eradicate. There are many reasons why the second society would have less diverse immune systems. In plants and animals, the farther the members of a species reside from the origin of that species in geographic space, the less genetic diversity they tend to exhibit. This statistical regularity arises because populations far from the source tend to have had relatively few founders.[59]

Consider one scenario of this binary model of immunity. It shows how a virus can become an epidemic.

Scenario 1: *The members of the first society bring three random viruses of length five and the members of the second society bring a single virus of length five.* From above, the probability that a virus from the first society cannot be killed by the common component of the second society's immune system equals $\frac{24}{32}$.[60] This means that of the three viruses carried by the first society, on average about two of them will have the potential to be epidemics. If not killed by the common component, they will not be killed by an individual's other four components with probability $\frac{4}{24}$, or $\frac{1}{6}$. The odds of an individual surviving both epidemics is $(\frac{1}{6})^2$, or about 3 percent.

To compute how many members of the first society die from viruses contracted from the second society, we first note that the probability of the entire first society being immune equals $\frac{4}{32}$. The probability that an individual can stop a potential epidemic is $\frac{10}{28}$, much higher than in the previous case. On average about one third of the first society will survive any potential epidemic.

In historical cases where few or no members of one society die from viruses carried by the other, it probably makes sense to think of these viruses as being much less complex—of much shorter length. This model with viruses of varying lengths, though it fits nicely with Diamond's account of the co-evolution of viruses and immune systems is overly simplistic. Nevertheless, it drives home a key lesson: more diversity implies greater responsiveness.

The Law of Requisite Variety

In analyzing immune systems, I made the straightforward argument that for a community to survive, for any virus, there must exist some member of the community that does not succumb. This logic can be extended into Ashby's *Law of Requisite Variety* (Ashby 1956), which originated in the field of system dynamics. The law of requisite variety applies to situations that require responses to external perturbations. Imagine waiting for something bad to happen and then having the responsibility of fixing what went wrong. Proactive maneuvers are not allowed. All choices are reactive to external stimuli. The law of requisite variety states that for every perturbation, there must exist an action to counter it.

Consider the task of keeping a bathtub in working order. One thing that could go wrong with this bathtub is that the faucet washers on the spigot could wear out. Call this event a *disturbance*. If a washer wears out, you fix it. Call this a *response*.

One day, unexpectedly, the drain springs a leak, a second disturbance. If you do nothing, you get a wet floor. If you take your one possible action—replacing the washer, you also get a wet floor. Changing the washer won't fix the problem. Instead, you have to patch the hole in the drain. The second disturbance needs a second response. This is the law of requisite variety.

Action/Disturbance	Worn Washer	Leaky Drain
Replace Washer	no drips	wet floor
Patch Hole	dripping faucet	dry floor

The Law of Requisite Variety

Let $D_1, D_2, \ldots, D_M$ be *disturbances* to a system that have distinct implications for performance. Let $R_1, R_2, \ldots, R_N$ be *responses*.

Law of Requisite Variety: *The number of responses, N, should equal the number of disturbances, M.*

The law of requisite variety provides an insight into well-functioning complex systems. The diversity of potential responses must be sufficient to handle the diversity of disturbances. If disturbances become more diverse, then so must the possible responses. If not, the system won't hold together. These responses aren't just sitting on a shelf. They must be generated, and generating potential responses is costly. Over time, the number of responses generated should tend to equal the number of disturbances because those responses that never get evoked should atrophy.

Consider raising a child. Young children produce approximately four types of disturbances: *hungry, wet, tired,* and *sick*. These require four responses: *feed, change, put in car seat and drive around town for two hours,* and *take to the doctor*. As children get older, the number of disturbances grows, and the number of responses must grow accordingly. A teenager disturbed by a relationship issue won't be calmed by one of those four responses (though food may help). The law of requisite variety states that the parent must develop new responses to counteract the new types of disturbances.

Example: Responsiveness in Organizations: I want to return to the idea of the economy as a complex system. Organizations within the economy must satisfy something like the law of requisite variety. In the strategy literature, the tasks that an organization executes well are referred to as its *core competencies*. These core competencies can be thought of as responses. If these responses are well suited to the likely disturbances, then the organization should be successful. No matter what the world offers up, the firm can handle it. If, on the other hand, an organization lacks sufficient core competencies, it may be headed for disaster. Again, if you only have a washer, you'll have a tough time fixing a leaky drain.

Prahalad and Bettis (1986) argue that the limits of firm diversification depend on whether the management team can respond to strategic variety across subunits. When one firm acquires another, the management team of the acquiring firm must be able to respond to the types of strategic issues that arise within the acquired firm. So long as the newly acquired firm has a set of disturbances similar enough to those of the original firm, all is well. For every disturbance, there exists a response.

If, however, the new disturbances differ from the acquiring firm's existing set of disturbances, the takeover may be a disaster. The acquiring firm may lack the requisite response variety. The lesson would seem obvious: *do not acquire businesses that require different skill sets.* Harley Davidson, for example, should not buy Kroger, a grocery store chain, because Harley Davidson's core competencies might not include responses that pertain to food spoilage.

This same logic applies to almost any complex system. A household is a complex system—diverse entities interacting in space and time. Consider what happens when friends or relatives come to visit your family. The visitors create a new set of disturbances: lines for the bathroom, no more milk in the fridge, or long stories told at the dinner table. If your family has not have developed enough responses, that is, core competencies, to handle these disturbances, the result may be a fractious, unhappy household. In households that frequently invite guests, core competencies evolve that prove capable of withstanding any disturbance, including guests who take forty-five-minute showers.

Whether the damage created by insufficient responses can be contained depends on a depth of analysis that lies beyond the scope of this book. Such an investigation would touch on big questions like why we see mass extinctions. This question has long captivated paleontologists. Massive system level effects such as these may well arise because the system cannot respond. But why? Is it due to lack of responsiveness or the size of the effect? Erwin (2001) describes six potential causes of the Permian-Triassic extinction. These include singular events—meteor impacts and volcanic disruptions— and big subtle changes—the formation of Pangaea (a single landmass) and a drop in sea levels. Whatever happened, the system lacked the appropriate response and the result was not pretty.

Competition

Complex systems, especially economies and political systems, require competition in order to flourish. Competition prevents firms from becoming inefficient and creates a strong incentive for innovation. In democracies, the absence of competition can lead to corruption (Gryzmala-Busse 2007). As previously mentioned, economists and political scientists use the *diversity index* as a measure of competition. Recall that the diversity index captures both the number of entities and their sizes. In the economic context, the higher the number of firms, the more competitive the market, and the more the consumers benefit. In the political context, the analysis is more nuanced. Too many parties can lead to confusion. And, depending on the electoral institution, more parties—as measured by the diversity index—need not mean better electoral outcomes for voters. In politics, then, more isn't necessarily better, but most political scientists believe that two is probably better than one. That's because competition drives out corruption, gives voice to diverse interests, and induces innovation.

The clearest case for the benefits of competition can be found in markets. The linkage between the number of firms and benefits to consumers is straightforward in many cases. Consider a market in which the producers sell identical products, or what are called commodities. If the firms compete over price, then two firms will be sufficient to drive price to marginal cost. This is known as *Bertrand Competition*. The resulting low price benefits consumers.

If, instead, firms compete by making quantity choices, so called *Cournot Competition*, the story becomes more nuanced. As more firms enter the market, the total amount produced rises. This happens even though firms are aware of how many firms are in the market. The logic is fairly subtle. Let's start with a monopolist. A monopolist wants to maintain a high price. Therefore, it holds back on production. When a second firm enters, that firm too wants to maintain a high price. However, the two firms will produce more of the good than the monopolist, because each firm has only half the market and suffers only half the consequences when the price falls from increasing production.

This effect is most easily seen in an example. Suppose that when production increases from 100 units to 110 units the price falls from $10 to $9. A monopolist will hold production at 100 units because total revenues are higher ($1000 versus $990). But if there are two firms, each selling 50 units, if one increases its output to 60, then its revenue increases (from $500 to $540). Provided that increase in revenue exceeds the costs of making the extra goods the firm will choose to make 60 units.

This same logic hold as the number of firms increases. The existence of more firms implies more production, lower prices, and greater market efficiency. What's worth noting here is that this argument does not rely on any diversity of the firms. The firms sell identical products. It's not the diversity of types that creates competition but the number of autonomous decision makers.

It's important here to distinguish between a *commodity* and a *differentiated product*. As mentioned above, a commodity, say #2 red wheat, is a good that has no relevant

differences for the market. My #2 red wheat is the same
as Sadie's wheat from the neighboring farm. Therefore, the
price I can charge is the same as the price she can charge.
Differentiated products, such as Ford and GM cars, may
be similar but they are not identical. With differentiated
products, firms have some market power based on their
differences.

Competition, then, works as a force for diversity. Producers don't want their goods to become commodities because
they then lose the ability to charge high prices. Producers
use techniques like advertising and packaging to encourage
diverse preferences. Diverse preferences create markets for
differentiated products.

With differentiated products, increasing the number of
firms has three effects. First, as before, more competition
means lower prices. Second, the existence of more firms
implies that the diverse tastes of consumers will be better
met by the market's offering. Third, the existence of more
(and diverse) firms offers all the advantages of diversity
that we've covered so far. To take just one, if firms differ
in their production processes, say by using different raw
materials, then the industry will be more robust owing to this
diversity.

Competition also can be seen as a selective pressure.
Absent competition, entities—be they firms, species, political
parties, or ideas—may lack pressure to improve or respond to
changes on the landscape. Diversity, insofar as it means more
actors, means more competition. Diversity, insofar as it means
differentiation and finding one's niche, implies less pressure.
Then again, diversity provides the seeds for innovation and
thus pulls back in the other direction, toward more pressure.

To put a bow on this discussion, systems need competition to flourish, and diversity increases competition.

Synergies I: Superadditivity

I now turn to ways in which diversity can produce innovations and improvements in performance. I start by describing superadditivity. A function f is said to be *superadditive* if $f(x+y) \geq f(x) + f(y)$. In other words, the whole exceeds the sum of the parts. I describe three examples of superadditivity. The first concerns the evapotranspiration of a wetland. The second involves what biologists call *synergistic epistasis*, and the third demonstrates how combinations of heuristics solve problems.

Suppose that we want to measure the evaporation in a wetland with two hundred lily plants in two thousand gallons of water. We can measure the evaporation of a potted plant, and we can measure the evaporation from a pan containing a gallon of water. We can then multiply the first number by two hundred and the second number by two thousand and add the two numbers together to get an estimate of the evaporation for the entire system. That estimate will be low. The water and the plants together evaporate more water than either the plants or the water would do alone. The reason isn't deep. The evaporation from the water increases ambient humidity, allowing the lilies to evaporate more efficiently (Kay 2008).

In biology, mutations can produce similar synergistic effects. Suppose that one mutation produces stronger tree roots and a second mutation produces taller trees. The first mutation alone would be nice, but probably unnecessary. The second mutation alone would lead to trees that fall down. The two mutations together produce *synergistic epistasis* (in layperson's terms, an interaction that is beneficial): a tall tree that won't fall down.

To show how heuristics are superadditive, I start simple. Suppose that you have a jar that you cannot open. You may know two tricks for opening jars. You can heat the lid to expand it or you can bang the top of the jar on the table to get it unstuck. If you know these two tricks you also know a third trick, namely, to heat the lid *and* bang it on the table. One plus one equals three!

This logic extends. If we know k ways to tackle a problem, then we can often apply those k distinct ways in combination. If we let $f(k)$ characterize the number of possible combinations of methods to solving a problem, we get that $f(k) = 2^k - 1$, which is by definition, superadditive.[61]

The power of superadditivity explains how given some rather mild assumptions, diverse groups of people may outperform groups of the best individuals (Hong and Page 2004; Page 2007). To show the basic logic, I ignore all of the details of how groups interact. In this model, there are N points on a circle numbered from 1 to N. Each point has a value in $[0, 100]$ assigned according to a nonlinear function. Each agent has a set of three distinct problem-solving tricks called *heuristics*. Each heuristic j is a number in the set $\{1, 2, \ldots, 20\}$. These numbers represent how far to look ahead on the circle. Therefore, it is possible to identify an agent by an ordered set of three integers $\{i, j, k\}$, where $i, j, k \in \{1, 2, 20\}$. Given these assumptions, there exist $6,840$ possible problem solvers.

For convenience, I assume that search for the best solution always begins at the point labeled number one.[62] If the agent's heuristics are {7, 11, 13}, then the agent compares the value at one with the values at eight, twelve, and fourteen sequentially. In other words, the agent looks ahead seven, eleven, and thirteen spots on the circle. If any of these points have higher values, the agent moves to that point and again applies her heuristics. If not, the agent is stuck on a *local optimum*.[63]

The *ability* of an agent can be captured by how well the agent performs working on a problem by itself. We can therefore rank all 6,840 agents according to their ability. Now, we might think that the best individual agents make up the best team, but that's not necessarily the case. To see why a diverse team may outperform a team of the best individuals requires thinking in terms of diversity and not in terms of ability. If the size of a circle denotes ability, then the two groups would look as shown in figure 8.2:

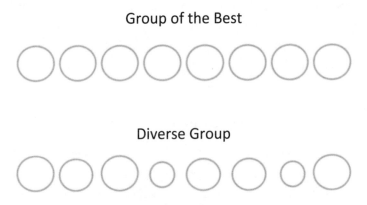

Figure 8.2. Abilities of Best Group and Diverse Group.

If we represent these groups by their heuristics, we get figure 8.3:

Group of the Best

Diverse Group

Figure 8.3. Heuristics of Best and Diverse Groups.

The union of the set of heuristics is much larger for the second group. In other words, the second group has more diversity.[64] Weitzman (1998) takes these ideas one step farther and shows how combining ideas can produce economic growth. The resulting model of what he calls *recombinant growth* relies on the fact that even a relatively modest number of ideas produces many combinations. If even a fraction of those combinations bear fruit, then the economy can continue to innovate and grow.[65]

Synergies II: Multiple Landscapes

In the earlier discussion of exploration and exploitation, I showed how exploration is necessary in a complex system. When the landscape dances, entities must respond if they hope to survive. Successful exploration can be thought of as innovation. An alternative spin on that entire discussion is that sustained innovation is crucial to a well functioning complex system.

In the previous section, I showed how diverse tools and tricks can be combined to form even more tricks. Here, I describe a second driver of innovation in complex systems: *diverse representations*. Recall that I covered diverse representations as a cause of diversity in Chapter 4. Here, I make two straightforward and related points. First, I show that what is difficult in one representation may be obvious in another (Page 2007; van Someren et al. 1998). Second, I show that with sufficient representational diversity, any problem can be solved.

I make the first point with an example. Suppose I ask you to give me the next number in the following sequence:

$$11 \quad 22 \quad 33 \quad 110$$

You might well be stumped. But suppose that I gave you this sequence instead:

$$5 \quad 10 \quad 15 \quad 20$$

In this case, the next number would be obvious to anyone. It's 25. It turns out that the first sequence also consists of the numbers 5, 10, 15, and 20. They're just written in base four and not in the usual base ten. The next number will be 25 in base four, which equals 121. This example shows that what is obvious in one representation may not be so obvious in another. Thus, having multiple ways to look at a problem can be beneficial.

To make my second point, that with enough representational diversity any problem can be solved easily, I need to return to the notion of an adaptive landscape. In genetic evolution, there exists a single landscape encoded by genes. In the constructed world of social, political, and economic problems, that landscape depends on a representation. If we have two different representations, then we have two different landscapes. Each adaptive landscape has local peaks. If the landscapes differ, then a local peak on one landscape need not be a local peak on another. The only solution that necessarily is a local peak on every landscape is the global optimum. In the box below, I formalize this intuition.

Diverse Representations and Local Optima

Assume that there exist a finite set X of size n of possibilities and an objective function $F : X \rightarrow [0, 100]$. Let $P^i(N) \rightarrow X$ be a representation that maps the set of integers $N = \{1, 2, \ldots, n\}$ into X. Define the local optima of P^i, given F, to be any point that has a higher value than its predecessor and successor as

$$L(P^i, F) = \{s \in N : F(P^i(s - 1)) \leq F(P^i(s)) \geq F(P^i(s + 1))\}$$

The local optima for a set of diverse representations $P = \{P^1, P^2, \ldots, P^m\}$ can be written as:

$$L(P, F) = \bigcap_{i=1}^{m} L(P^i, F)$$

Taking this logic—that the only place a collection can get stuck is at an intersection of their local peaks—to the extreme yields the following result: with sufficient diversity in representations, the only common local peak will be the optimal solution.

Synergies III: Diversity Production

To show the final synergistic effect of diversity, diversity production, I return to the immune system model from above in which viruses are binary strings of length five. Consider a world in which all possible immune systems are present. Suppose that virus 00 appears on the scene, followed quickly by virus 11. The following eighteen immune systems will remain in the population after the first virus:

Survivors of 00: 00000, 00001, 00011, 00010, 00100, 00101, 00110, 00111, 01000, 01001, 01100, 10000, 10001, 10010, 10011, 11000, 11001, 11100

Of these eighteen, eight will also survive an attack by 11.

Survivors of 00 and 11: 00011, 00110, 00111, 01100, 10011, 11000, 11001, 11100

These eight immune systems are quite diverse: at each of the five locations there are exactly four 1s and four 0s in the population. Also, at any two locations, say the first and the third, all four possible pairs of 0 and 1 are present: 00, 01, 10, and 11. Finally, when we look at sets of three locations, we see that six of the eight possible combinations: everything except 010 and 101 is present.

Assume that immune systems are carried over during reproduction as described earlier when we covered the evolution
of diversity. This diversity within the population allows for
the production of diversity through recombination. Suppose
that immune system 00011 is crossed with 11100. There
are four places where recombination can occur. If we walk
through each one, we see that they will very likely create a
new string. If they switch initial bits, they become 10011
and 01101; the latter does not belong to the surviving set.
If the recombination occurs at the first two locations, they
become 11011 and 00100, neither of which belongs to the
surviving set. If they cross at the third location, they become
00000 and 11111, systems that are also not part of the set.
Finally, if they cross at the fourth location, they become,
00001 and 11110, neither of which belongs to the surviving
set. This example demonstrates how a diverse set can ramp up
its diversity through recombination.

Collective Knowledge

The next effect of diversity that I discuss is collective knowledge. Before I start, I need to distinguish between data (symbols and signals), information (organized data), knowledge
(an understanding of how information fits together), and
wisdom (the intelligence to know which knowledge to apply
in which setting) (Rowley 2007). Collective knowledge refers
to the ability of a collective to come to an accurate forecast or
to decide on an optimal action.[66]

I am going to focus here on how groups of people produce
collective knowledge. Each person or species sees only part
of the world. This claim holds true in two senses. We're

limited geographically in what we see, and we're limited in our capacities to take in information. We therefore rely on categories. We coarse grain reality into partitions. In formal terms, a partition divides a set into disjoint subsets. A division of fauna by number of legs is a partition. Here's where diversity enters. If we partition reality differently, then we make different predictions. If we individually make different predictions, then collectively, we can be accurate.

Collective knowledge occurs in the animal world as well. Bee colonies exploit diverse information to identify food sources (Seeley 1996). Ants drop pheromone trails that lead to efficient routes between food sources (Gordon 1999). These pheromone trails are a form of *stigmercy*: a process by which a species leaves a mark on the environment that can be used as information. Bison trails are another examples. Bison trample grass leaving clues for other bison, and eventually humans, to follow (Johnson 2003).

To show how diversity produces collective knowledge requires two steps. Step one is showing that diverse partitions lead to different forecasts or predictions. Step two is showing that diverse individual predictions create accurate collectives. The logic for how diverse partitions lead to different predictions is relatively straightforward. Suppose that that we're trying to predict which berries in the forest are poisonous. One person might categorize the berries by color. Another person might categorize them by size. A third might categorize them by firmness. To keep this example as simple as possible, I consider two colors (red and blue), two sizes (small and large), and two degrees of firmness (hard and soft). Each of these categorizations divides the set of berries into two sets. And

provided there exists a diverse set of types of berries, these
categories will differ: if all eight types of berries are possible—
from small hard red berries to large soft blue berries, then
these categorizations will differ.

The number of possible partitions is enormous and is
known as *Bell's Number.*

Bell's Number: The Number of Partitions

Given a set with N members, the number of partitions
of that set, B_N, is given by the following recursive
function: $B_0 = B_1 =$ and for all successive N:

$$B_{N+1} = \sum_{i=0}^{N} \binom{N}{i} B_i$$

Therefore, $B_2 = 2$, $B_3 = 5$, $B_4 = 15$, $B_5 = 52$,
$B_6 = 203$, $B_7 = 877$, $B_8 = 4140$, $B_9 = 21,147$, and
$B_{10} = 115,975$.

This incredibly large number of partitions implies enormous potential diversity in categorizations of reality and,
perforce, diversity in possible models. Each person with a
different partition has a different predictive model. One such
model might be "soft berries are safe, and hard berries are
poisonous." Another model might be "blue berries are safe,
and red berries are poisonous."

The second step in the logic relates diversity in individual
predictions to collective accuracy. In a previous book, I refer
to this as the *Diversity Prediction Theorem* (Page 2007).

Diversity Prediction Theorem

Assume N individuals make predictions about the value of some outcome. Let v equal the true value of an outcome and let s_i be the prediction of person i, so that the collective prediction is $\bar{s} = \frac{1}{N}\sum_{i=1}^{N} s_i$. The following equality holds:

$$(v - \bar{s})^2 = \sum_{i=1}^{N}(v - s_i)^2 - \sum_{i=1}^{N}(\bar{s} - s_i)^2,$$

which can be stated as

Collective Error = Average Individual Error−Prediction Variance

---

The diversity prediction theorem shows how diversity and ability contribute to collective knowledge. Diversity in predictive models creates variation in predictions. And, predictive variance matters just as much as average ability in producing collective knowledge.[67]

Redundancy and Degeneracy

I now introduce a simple but powerful idea: if a system contains redundant parts, then it will be more robust to the failure of one of the parts. This logic applies to a firm that has two employees capable of performing a task or to a transportation system that contains multiple routes between two locations. Redundancy comes with costs as well. Most systems have fixed capacity. This constraint produces a *redundancy-diversity tradeoff*. Increase redundancy too much and you sacrifice diversity. Eradicate all redundancies and you wind up with a fragile system.

Biologists distinguish between two types of redundancy that I'll call *pure redundancy* and *degeneracy*. By pure redundancy, I mean literally having multiple copies of the same part. Those extra flashlight batteries in a drawer in the laundry room are purely redundant. Degeneracy refers to structures that physically differ yet can perform the same task or fulfill the same function. If I build a fire on a beach, a bucket of sand and a bucket of water would be degenerate solutions to the problem of putting out the fire.

Edelman and Gally (2001) demonstrate that degeneracy is a "ubiquitous biological property." By that they mean that you can choose any level: population, individual, cellular, or genetic, and you'll find degeneracy. An excellent example of degeneracy occurs in the genetic code. When I described neutral mutations in Chapter 3, I gave a stylized example of multiple representations of the same phenotype and showed how that enabled greater search. Here, I provide greater detail to show how degeneracy promotes robustness.

I begin with some basic genetics. The double helix structure of human DNA consists of four nucleotide bases: adenine (abbreviated A), cytosine (C), guanine (G), and thymine (T). These bases form triplets of base pairs that code for twenty amino acids. Were there no constraints, the number of triplets of pairs would equal $4^6 = 4096$. But each member of a base pair has a unique partner, which reduces this number of triplets of pairs to sixty-four. These sixty-four triplets of pairs produce only twenty amino acids: lysine, glutamine, alanine, etc. Thus, different triplets must produce identical amino acids. On average, then, more than three triplets of pairs (different structures) produce each amino acid.

To go back to my earlier example of the beach fire, to achieve a ratio of three to one would require adding a beach blanket to the bucket of sand and the pail of water. We might think that a ratio of three to one seems like a substantial amount of degeneracy. But we have to keep in mind that this was the degeneracy ratio for a single amino acid. A sequence of just ten amino acids would have a degeneracy ratio of three raised to the tenth power, or almost 60,000 distinct structures that produce that sequence. To go back to our beach fire, even if we enlisted all 52,400 fire departments in the United States, we wouldn't have that level of degeneracy.[68]

Increasing redundancy and degeneracy enhances robustness. Better to have two smoke alarms rather than one, in the event that one fails. Even better, though, to have two different types of alarms—one that responds to smoke and one to heat. Bednar (2009) makes this point about robust political systems. The checks on government encroachment include the courts and the people. These checks respond to distinct, but correlated stimuli. If the executive branch grabs power it can be reined in on constitutional grounds or through citizen uprising.

Redundancy also makes transportation systems more robust. In 1994, I was living in southern California. Early one morning, I was awakened by what is now known as the Northridge Earthquake. The highway system around Los Angeles suffered major damage. Several highways had at least one bridge collapse. Yet, daily traffic flows in Los Angeles continued, though not quite unabated. The network proved robust. Drivers continued to be able to get from point A to point B because of multiple paths between locations and because even where a bridge did collapse, traffic was rerouted around the bridge.

Not all transportation systems are as robust. The pass between Yosemite National Park and Lake Tahoe closes for the winter when the heavy snows begin. Once that road closes, automobile traffic between those locations reduces substantially because the only alternative routes involve hundreds of miles of travel. The lack of redundancy hinders system performance.

In systems with capacity constraints a tradeoff arises between redundancy and diversity. Greater diversity entails more responsiveness—think back to the law of requisite variety—but increases the odds that the failure of any one entity could cause the system to collapse. Greater redundancy implies less ability to respond to new disturbances but a greater ability to withstand the loss of any one entity in the system. On balance, a system must trade off redundancy with diversity much in the same way it trades off exploitation (doing what it does well) and exploration (continuing to look for something better). Redundancy guarantees that the system can keep doing what it's doing. Diversity enables it to respond to new disturbances.

In systems that are not so constrained by capacity, the field tilts in the direction of greater diversity. Viruses, which have enormous populations, have fewer built in redundancies in their genetic code than do mammals. This results in more phenotypic variation among viruses. Viruses can afford to sacrifice members of their population because they can reproduce so quickly (Krakauer and Plotkin 2002). Humans cannot. Hence, our phenotypes are more robust.

To expand on some of these ideas relating to pure redundancy, degeneracy, and robustness, I present three examples, one involving food webs, one about supply chains, and one that concerns the Internet. In each example, I show the relationship between diversity and system performance. To make the reading less jargon laden, I use the term redundancy to refer to both pure redundancy and degeneracy.

Example #1 Ecologies and Food Webs: I first show how food webs have redundancy. In a food web, the objects are species, and a connection implies that one species eats the other. Therefore, in one sense food webs are unidirectional. If we follow a food web down to its final nodes, we find species that get their energy from some primitive source: the soil, freshwater, seawater, the sun, or some combination of these things. Species farther up the food chain consume the same energy after it has been transformed by other species.

As described earlier, in food webs, species can be crudely classified according to their trophic level. This classification into trophic levels places a hierarchical structure on who eats whom. Consider the picture of a food web in figure 8.4. There are three trophic levels. Four species exist at the lowest level, three at the middle level, and two at the top level. Each species at one trophic level eats species at the level below it. The species at the lowest level are the only species that have direct access to the energy source, but all species have multiple paths to that energy.

Suppose that a species at one of those levels became extinct. This would undoubtedly have an effect on the population sizes within the food web. The other species at the same level might grow in population size, as might the species at the level below it (if that level exists). If there exists a level above it, the populations at that level might decrease in population owing to the reduction in the number of prey.

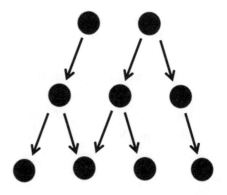

Figure 8.4. Food web with three trophic levels.

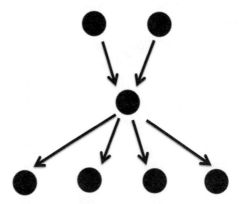

Figure 8.5. A Food web with a single species at the second trophic level.

Now consider a second food web (Figure 8.5) in which there is a single species in the middle trophic level. If this species were to become extinct, the species in the level above it would do so as well. The species in the level below it would grow unchecked. In the ecology literature, the sole species in the second level would be called a *keystone species*. If it gets wiped out, the ecology fails.

The first food web is obviously more robust than the second one. A reasonable hypothesis would seem to be that the more connections in a food web, the more robust the food web should be to extinctions. Before, jumping to that conclusion, five caveats are in order. First, real world food webs are not connected between trophic levels like our first model, nor are they isolated on a single trophic level except at the top. Real food webs are much more complicated than these. Second, species can adapt. This is called phenotypic plasticity. Species can change what they eat. Behavioral changes can be even more extreme than diet. If an ecosystem contains too few male groupers, the largest female grouper becomes a male (Low 2001).

Third, if new connections can be formed, the number of latent or possible connections may be more important than the ones we see in a picture of a food web. Fourth, once the other species adapt in response to the loss of a species, the resulting food web differs. If a diurnal species responds to a disturbance by becoming nocturnal, the web could look very different. Comparing the food web after a species has been knocked out with the original food web would be akin to comparing apples to oranges. Finally, the robustness of food webs refers not only to robustness to extinction but also to robustness to invasion. More connections could imply a similarity of attributes that allows an invading parasite to eradicate an entire trophic level.

Example #2 Supply Chains: The idea that multiple paths lead to more robust networks also applies to supply chains. Supply chains are used to provide parts for sophisticated products like an airplane or an MRI machine. If a firm has only a single way to get a specific part, the firm suffers two consequences. First, network breakdown can occur. If some connection along that single path collapses, the firm can be forced to shut down. The unique supplier of the part will be just like a keystone species. Such shutdowns can be costly. In 2001, following the September 11th terrorist attacks, the Ford Motor Company shut down five American plants for a week owing to delays in getting some parts across the Canadian border, losing millions of dollars.

Second, if a firm that has a unique supplier of a part may have to pay a high prices as the supplier will realize that it has market power. As was the case with food webs, supply chains are complex. They must be robust to labor strikes, weather, terrorist attacks, power outages, earthquakes, price shifts, and raw material shortages. Different supply chains face different types and frequencies of disturbances, rendering it difficult to make any sweeping statements about what makes a network fragile or robust.

Example #3 The Internet and the WWW: Some networks, like the Internet (the network of computers) and the World Wide Web (the network of information on those computers) have a power law distribution of connections. Recall from our discussion of the central limit theorem that a power law distribution implies many small events and a handful of very large events. Power laws can arise in many situations. In networks, they may arise because of preferential attachment. Under preferential attachment, new connections attach to an object in proportion to the number of connections an object already has (Barabási 2003).

For the Internet and the World Wide Web, robustness corresponds to connectedness. If the computers are all connected, the network functions. If they are not connected, information cannot flow between them. The same notion of robustness applies to power grids and systems of roads. For these networks to function properly, all objects must be connected.

I cover power law networks in order to make a point about how robustness depends on assumptions about behavior. My treatment will be brief, as Barabási (2003) makes this argument clearly and in great detail. Suppose, first, that the Internet suffers random failures of computers. With a power law distribution of connections, these failures will probably not render the network disconnected because most computers are only connected to a couple of other computers. The only way that a few hundred random failures would cause the graph of the network to lose connectedness would be for those random failures to hit the handful of most connected computers, a highly unlikely event. Extending this logic, we would expect a power law distribution of connections to be more robust than a uniform distribution of connections.[69] And in fact, this has been shown to be true by Barabási and others.

Suppose instead that the failures are not random but strategic. A strategic failure can be thought of as an attack. An intelligent attack would target the most connected computers. If those computers failed, the network might become disconnected. Owing to the number of highly connected nodes in a network with a power law distribution, those networks would be less robust than random networks to strategic attack.

I want to extend this intuition to make a larger point. Suppose that I begin with a network in which each object is connected to approximately the same number of other objects. I then increase the diversity in the number of connections by making some small subset of the objects more connected and most of the objects less connected. This increase in connectedness diversity has two effects. It makes the network more robust to random failures because most objects have fewer connections. It also makes the network less robust to strategic failures because an attack can focus on the connected objects. This insight provides yet another example of why we must be careful not to make broad statements like "diversity implies robustness." Some types of diversity increase some forms of robustness and simultaneously reduce other types of robustness.

Redundancy and Robustness of Communication

Applying the multiple paths idea to the robustness of informational systems requires a different model. In the previous cases, we cared only that the network remained connected. Multiple paths were a form of insurance for the failure of an object or a connection in the network. In organizations that process information, multiple paths reduce error in message passing.[70] To see how this works, we consider a variant of the telephone game. In the telephone game, people sit in a circle. An originator sends a message to the person sitting on her left. That person tells the same message to the person on his left. The message continues being passed until it gets returned to the originator. Errors accrue over time and the message that the originator hears may differ substantially from the one she sent.

The ability to give clear concise instructions that cannot be misinterpreted is an extremely valuable skill, even in today's highly connected economy. In the past, people could not pick up a cell phone and say "What did you mean?" The ability to communicate clearly was crucial. Among other talents, Ulysses S. Grant, the Civil War general, was renowned for his clean writing style. Waging war at that time required unambiguous messages so that conditional actions could be coordinated across time and place. Grant's memoirs are considered a classic in American literature.

To see what could go wrong in the telephone game, I construct a modern day version using the online translator Babel Fish. In my version, I start with a message in English, translate it to Dutch, and then from Dutch to French. I then translate to German and then the German back into English. The following diagram shows the sequence of translations:

English → Dutch → French → German → English

If I take the first stanza from the Star Spangled Banner, here is the sequence of messages produced:

English: Oh say can you see, by the dawn's early light

Dutch: Oh zegt kan u, door dawn' zien; s vroeg licht

French: Oh dit vous, pouvez par dawn' ; voir ; s lève tôt

German: Sie können durch dawn' so genanntes Oh; ; siehe; s früh auf heben Sie

English: They can by dawn' Oh so called; see; early on lift you

All fun aside, the fact that I consider only a single path allows for the errors to accumulate. If I go from English to French to Dutch and back to English I get

English: Oh said can see you, by dawn' ; first lifts of s

If presented with both final sentences, many people could infer the original message. But from either message alone, most people would not have any idea what was being communicated. If you play the Babel Fish version of the telephone game with various network structures, you will see how multiple paths create greater robustness.

Better though to show how errors accumulate with a model. The model will involve passing up a message that is a simple binary signal: Yes or No. I assume that an organizational structure is a hierarchical network that has levels. A person at the lowest level hears the true signal. She repeats that signal to the person or persons at the next level. There is some small probability that a mistake in communication occurs. If this occurs, the person at the second level thinks the signal is No, when in fact the true signal was Yes. For the purposes of this example, I assume that the probability of such an error is 5 percent.

The probability that the correct signal reaches the top level can be written as a function of the number of levels and the number of independent paths. Suppose, for example, that there are four levels and one path. With four levels the message must be passed three times, so there are three opportunities for errors. The probability that no errors are made is 95 percent times 95 percent times 95 percent or about 86 percent. The probability that an error is made in the communication between the first and second levels but not between the other two levels equals 5 percent times 95 percent times 95 percent or 4.5 percent. The same calculation implies that the probability of an error only between levels two and three and three and four also equals 4.5 percent. Therefore, there is a 13.5 percent chance of the wrong message arriving at the top level due to a single error. If two errors are made the correct signal makes it to the top (though only by luck). The probability of this happening can be shown to be less than 1 percent. The probability of three errors occurring is even smaller.

Alternatively, suppose that the organization sent the information up through three different paths. From our previous calculation, we know that there is about at 86 percent chance that it will be correct and about a 14 percent chance that it will be wrong. However, the correctness of these messages will be independent. So, each message should be more likely than not to be correct, but there is some chance that the messages will not agree. Therefore, the person at the top of the hierarchy should just assume that whichever message occurs more often is the true signal. The probability that all three of the messages will be the same and correct is about 64 percent. The probability that two of the three messages will be the same and correct equals about 31 percent. Therefore the person at the top of the hierarchy can make the correct inference about 95 percent of the time.

We can construct a more general model in which there are L levels in the hierarchy and M paths. The more levels in the hierarchy, the more likely that an error will occur somewhere along the path. The more paths, the more likely that the more common message will be the same as the original signal. A diversity of paths leads to fewer errors. Again, we see a relationship between diversity of paths and robustness of the system.

We can extend this insight to draw some inferences about information transmission in society. If we have lots of diverse paths to an information source, we are not likely to make mistakes. If we only have a few paths, mistakes are likely. In the lead up to the second U.S.–Iraq war, mistakes occurred in the U.S. attempts to discern whether Iraq had weapons of mass destruction. Sources suggested that Iraq had such weapons. The U.S. did not have independent sources providing information. If it had, it may have realized the error. The government was not alone in making the wrong inference. On Sunday May 30, 2004, the *New York Times* editorial board admitted that they had also erred by not having enough independent means of verification.

Firewalling and Modularity

Diversity can also aid in the containment of disaster. It does so in two ways. The first is through modularization (Krakauer 2005). The importance of modularization for robustness is well-covered territory (Levin 2000). Modularization restricts damage to a single component. The failure of an individual component can be damaging, but it's hardly a catastrophe. If redundant components fill the same functional role, the larger ecosystem will be unaffected.

Redundancy of clusters may be as important as the modularity. The human body is modular, but in places it lacks redundancy. If a person's heart fails, he's as good as dead. Unlike in an ecosystem, there's no other heart to step in an take its place. As a result, the failure spreads.

Parts of the human body are both modularized and have built in redundancy. The brain, for example, combines modularity and enough plasticity to produce redundancy (Fodor 1983). Injuries to some regions of the brain create bounded functional losses, not total cognitive breakdown. A person with damage to Broca's region may be unable to speak yet still be capable of processing information.

In light of the power of modularity and redundancy, engineered systems rely on those two properties as core design principles (Baldwin and Clark 2000). In modular systems, parts can be refined and even replaced. Any time we replace a car battery or transmission, we're exploiting the modularity of a car's design. Airplanes exploit modularity and redundancy. For many functions, pilots can turn off automated controls and take over their operation manually.

The second way diversity contains disasters is through firewalling. I'll show this in an example in which spatial patterns create firewalls in a model of susceptible, but diverse, entities in a line. To make this more tangible, suppose that these are oak, elm, and maple trees planted along a street. Assume that each type of tree is susceptible to attack by viruses, but the viruses that kill one type, say oaks, cannot attack the other species (elms and maples). To keep the model simple, assume that a virus occurs with some small probability

q at each location independently, and that with probability p it kills the tree at that location.

These assumptions roughly match reality. Viruses, fungi, or insects can attack trees. Viruses need a host to survive. Fungi can live on their own for short periods of time. They are self-sustaining living organisms. Some of the most lethal diseases, such as chestnut blight, which wiped out almost all of the chestnut trees in the United States, are fungi. Trees' immune systems generate pesticides that can eradicate these fungi, but in the case of the chestnut, the immune systems proved ineffective. The fungi won.

Dutch elm disease is also fungal. Insects carry Dutch elm disease, but it also spreads through root grafting. The insects, all too appropriately named elm bark beetles, lay eggs on dying elms, and their offspring carry the fungus to other trees. When spread by insects the fungus affects the trees differently than if the fungus spreads by root grafting. But in either case, the dissemination is localized. The root system of an elm might cross under a street, but it won't cross town.

In light of the empirical evidence, it's reasonable to assume that the virus spreads a fixed distance. I begin with some examples for the case of sixty trees with exactly twenty trees of each type. I assume that the probability that a tree gets attacked by a virus, q, equals $\frac{1}{100}$, and the probability that the virus kills the tree, p, equals 1. Finally, I assume that the virus kills all trees of that type within a distance of five.

Pure Segregation: Under pure segregation of the types, the oak trees would look as follows:

OOOOOOOOOOOOOOOOOOOO

The probability that any individual oak tree does not get attacked by a virus equals $\frac{99}{100}$. The probability that none get attacked therefore equals $(\frac{99}{100})^{20}$, which is 81.7 percent.

The next question to ask is how far the virus will spread. This is easy to answer. All of the oak trees will die. In the first wave, all trees a distance five or less will die. Deaths are indicated by Xs:

OOOOXXXXXXXXXXXOOOOOO

In the next wave, the neighbors of those trees die:

XXXXXXXXXXXXXXXXXXXO

In the final wave, the remaining tree dies.

Alternatively, I can consider the case of maximal diversity. Here the trees are arranged oak, elm, maple, oak, elm, maple, and so on.

Maximal Diversity: Maximal diversity would look as follows:

OEMOEMOEMOEMOEMOEMOEMOEMOEMOE MOEMOEMOE

Here again if any oak tree is attacked, all of the oak trees will again die, though not as quickly. To see why, suppose that a tree near the center is attacked:

OEMOEMOEMOEM**X**EMOEMO

In the next wave of attacks, only two other trees die:

OEMOEMOEMXEM**X**EMXEMO

In subsequent waves at most two trees die as well. But the killing never stops until all of the oak trees are dead. So diversity here does no good other than to slow the rate of transmission from a maximum of ten dead trees per wave in the segregation case to a maximum of two dead trees per wave under maximal diversity. This slowing of the spread could give arborists time to stop the spread through some other means.

Maximal diversity does not halt the spread of the attack. To prevent the disease from spreading, each oak tree must be separated by at least five trees. This cannot be done with only forty non-oaks and twenty oaks. The oaks can, though, be segregated into patches that contain the spread.

Patches: In the patches arrangement, we create clusters of oaks, elms, and maples of size two and three. Groups of size two alternate with groups of size three

OOOEEMMMOOEEEMMOOOEEMMMOOEEEMM

In this arrangement, if an oak tree gets attacked, the wave will be contained within the patch of size two or three trees:

OOOEEMMMOOEEEMM**XXX**EEMMMOOEEEMM

On average, only two-and-a-half trees from each patch die from an attack.

The patch arrangement is only optimal given our assumption about how the attack spreads. That cannot be known a priori. Therefore, we would be unwise to create such a regular arrangement of trees. If the virus mutated so that it could travel just one more tree, then once again the oak trees would all be killed. The most prudent arrangement may be have clusters of varying sizes with varying distances between them. In other words, we would like diversity at the level of clusters and spaces as opposed to diversity at tree level.

Crosscutting Cleavages

The final effect of diversity in complex systems that I consider is how diverse connections enable crosscutting cleavages, which may enhance internal robustness. Internal robustness refers to the ability of a system to withstand adaptations and experimentations by the parts of the systems. Crosscutting cleavages are diverse sets of coalitions. Within an organization, a group of diverse individuals may form coalitions based on race, gender, work group, hobbies, tenure, or rank. If these coalitions create distinct groups, the cleavages are crosscutting. If each division creates the same coalition—if all young black women work in accounting and enjoy playing bridge and earn low incomes and all older white men work in finance, play golf, and earn large salaries, then cleavages are not crosscutting.

What I want to capture here is how crosscutting cleavages can prevent dissolution. I'll do this with a very stark model. Assume that there are N issues or interests. On each of these N interests, assume there exist two possible positions 0 and 1. I set $N = 6$ in the examples below but the number could be much larger. The agents could be people, nations, firms, subunits of a firm, teams, schools, organizations, social movements, religions, or even ideologies. The first case has no crosscutting cleavages.

No Crosscutting Cleavages: *All agents have interests in the set* {000000, 111111}.

With no crosscutting cleavages, segregation has no costs. Each individual either wants all 1s or all 0s. If the two coalitions break apart, no individual suffers the loss of a set of connections. Alternatively, suppose that people have random connections.

Random Diversity: *Each agent's interest on each issue is randomly chosen with 0s and 1s equally likely.*

In this case, it would be difficult, if not impossible, for an agent to make a case for segregation. Suppose an agent proposes that the 000000's segregate. These agents share a majority of interests with interest types such as 000111, 001100, 10000, and so on. If this collection of people broke into two groups, then people would lose the opportunity to interact with some likeminded people.

These two extreme cases hint at how interesting the middle ground can be. A collection of people with a moderate amount of diversity of preferences may include some people who'd like to separate. Their incentives to do so depend upon the extent of crosscutting cleavages.

The idea that crosscutting cleavages may promote internal robustness is not new. Ross (1920) wrote, "A society, therefore, which is ridden by a dozen oppositions along lines running in every direction, may actually be less in danger of being torn with violence or falling to pieces than one split just along one line. For each new cleavage contributes to narrow the cross clefts, so that one might say that society is sewn together by its inner conflicts." Similarly, a case can be made that a lack of crosscutting cleavages, real or perceived, can lead to civil wars. To borrow Lincoln's imagery, "a house divided will not stand."

Thus, pluralism may promote stability, especially if pluralism implies what Miller (1983) calls *preference clusters.* Miller argues that stability may create pluralism (it's only safe for these clusters to pursue interests and policies when the system is stable). But, many scholars have argued that the causality goes the other way. The reasons for this conclusion vary. Pluralism may lead to moderate attitudes or behavior. It may lead to distributed outcomes in which everyone gets a little of what they want so that no one wants to upset the system.

Miller also makes a compelling and theoretically interesting argument, that puts a new twist on a long line of theory that shows that diverse interests produce policy instability. Some see the instability as leading to chaos. Miller argues that the instability may be a good thing. Policy changes reconfigure the set of winners and losers. This means that citizens who take it on the chin during one election cycle may be willing to stay within the system, hoping for change. Thus, paradoxically, instability in outcomes may produce a more robust political system by creating crosscutting cleavages.

Summary

In this chapter, I've covered some of the effects of diverse types within complex systems. These include two types of specialization, responsiveness and competitiveness; three types of synergies; collective knowledge, redundancy, degeneracy, modularity, and crosscutting cleavages. I conclude this chapter with two brief points. First, these aren't the only effects of diversity. I'm confident that readers will be able to construct lists of substantial effects that I've neglected to discuss.

Second, I want to hearken back to a point I made earlier about the value of models. Models make possible a formal analysis of the effects of diversity. The measures and the models allow us to unpack our statements about diversity and add precision to impressionistic claims. Those claims can then be tested empirically. So, rather than merely saying "diversity creates synergies" we can say "increasing the diversity index of the heuristics in a population increases the chances that when two people meet that they can create something new." We can then test that hypothesis formally.

9

PARTING THOUGHTS

The art of progress is to preserve order amid change and
to preserve change amid order.
—ALFRED NORTH WHITEHEAD

In this book, I have introduced definitions and measures
of diversity and relied on simple models to explore the
effects of diversity in complex systems. I've devoted less
time to empirical facts about levels of diversity in economic,
social, and biological systems. I chose that path not because
I deem the facts unimportant. To the contrary, I agree
with Deborah Gordon (2010) and others that advances in
complex systems research require deep, accurate empirical
investigations. However, given the breadth of the topic at
hand, I felt the best approach was to provide a common
vocabulary and to identify those effects of diversity that
transcend domain.

At this point, I want to return to an issue that I raised
in the introduction: whether we can gain anything from
an interdisciplinary approach such as this one. Person-
ally, I believe that ecologists do have something to teach
bankers and that bankers have something to teach ecologists

(May et al. 2008). I also believe that this cross fertilization of ideas is more likely to occur if scholars from different disciplines have a common understanding of definitions, assumptions, modes of analysis, and even notation. Including discipline-specific assumptions that enhance realism can extend core models to make them useful within disciplines.

For example, in the previous three chapters, I described models that show potential benefits of diversity—averaging, diminishing returns, synergies and so on. Those benefits occur in most complex systems and at most levels. To take those ideas into a specific domain, I would need to add more detail. In my own area of research, social science, actors have agency. They can choose to opt in or out of many situations. Social science models include agency, and this can affect results.

Let me push this farther to show the need for more detail. In the models demonstrating synergies created by diverse types in complex systems, these benefits accrue at the aggregate level. The system itself is more robust, more efficient, or more innovative if it contains the appropriate amount and kinds of diversity. If an actor in a complex system possesses agency, he cares not about whether the system performs better, but about whether he does better than in some alternative system. Self-interest and the common interest don't always align. Even if interactions among diverse individuals produce system level robustness and efficiency, the relevant actors may not choose to take actions in the collective interest.[71]

Thus, even if in the aggregate, synergies created by diverse types create a larger pie, the split of that pie must be equitable for all those diverse parts to want to remain. To take a specific example, diverse teams of workers may have advantages over homogeneous teams. By diverse teams, I mean teams whose members possess different cognitive skills (Page 2007). In such situations, the contributions of particular members of the team can depend on the order in which the individuals work on the problem (Hong and Page 2001). An individual who takes an action that allows another individual to make a large improvement may be under-appreciated and opt out.

I don't mean to be pessimistic. I'm merely pointing out a possible problem to realizing the benefits of diversity in some cases. Overall, I'm sanguine about the potential for diverse teams to stay together when they're producing good results. All else being equal, larger benefits to diversity should make the diverse individuals more likely to stick around and contribute, so the greater the synergies realized, the less likely the system falls apart. In addition, if cognitive diversity correlates with other types of diversity such as identity, then these teams produce cross cutting cleavages, which might help hold society together.

Agency is not the only difference between diverse groups of people and ecosystems, or for that matter between groups of people and the brain. Ecosystems and the brain have been assembled over long periods of time through evolutionary pressures. Diverse groups are often tossed together. They haven't had the benefit of selective pressures. Should we be surprised that they perform poorly? If we constructed an ecosystem by randomly tossing together some flora and fauna would we really expect it to function? Of course not. We'd expect an initial period of assembly and organization in which many species go extinct. Thus, leveraging diversity requires an understanding of assembly.

Attempts at sense making of the assembly process necessarily involve network thinking—drawing connections between the interacting types. Once we include networks in a model, we add in another layer of complexity, and a very useful one at that. Consider the introduction of a new breed of dog—say, the labradoodle. The labradoodle will be desired by some traditional labrador owners, some people who would have been poodle owners, and some people who liked other breeds or didn't like other types of dogs at all. The introduction of this new breed sets in motion a process of what Schumpeter (1942) called *creative destruction*, albeit a fairly mild one.

The introduction of the Internet, by way of contrast, sets in motion a much larger process of destruction and of further creation. Newspapers have folded. New online businesses such as eBay have sprung up, and new ways of doing business have emerged that exploit the capability of instant sharing of information. By considering the full network, we can begin to see how some innovations, such as the labradoodle, lie on the fringes and produce only modest repercussions, and how other innovations lie at the core and create large crashes (Jain and Krishna 2002).

How we put things together and what we introduce to the mix would seem to be central questions that must be answered. One approach to gaining a foothold is to seek out properties that, for lack of a better phrase, play well with others. In the context of physical space, the architect Christopher Alexander (2001) has done just that. He has identified fifteen fundamental properties (such as strong centers, gradients, and thick boundaries), that he believes necessary to produce systems that have life. Alexander's framework doesn't just identify the parts but looks with an empirical eye at how those parts fit together to produce sums that exceed the parts. Analogous thinking might enhance our understanding of financial markets, political systems, and ecologies.

In the end, we're left with an undeniable fact: the physical, ecological, economic, political, and social systems that we inhabit and interact with and within are complex and diverse. And though I've tried to stay away from normative claims, I think that we probably want them to remain so. A lack of complexity would mean either order or randomness, and I think we all prefer to live somewhere in the region in between. In my more hopeful moments, I think that complex systems might be capable of achieving that balance on their own. Systems with too little diversity become predictable. Predictable ordered systems can be exploited. Ordered systems create incentives for innovation. And, as we have seen, innovations cause landscapes to dance and increase the complexity of the system.

In contrast, systems with too much diversity may well produce either chaos or randomness. Either of these phenomena may encourage entities to slow down their rates of adaptation or simplify their strategies. If either happens, systems that are out of control may settle back into a happy, moderate level of complexity.

I fear, though, that I may be too optimistic. Jim Crutchfield (2009) persuasively argues that humans seem bent on adding more and more new ideas, instruments, and products generating more and more complexity. And we need only recall one of our definitions of complexity (the difficulty of predicting outcomes) along with one of the phenomena that complex systems produce (large events) to come face to face with what Crutchfield calls "hidden fragility."

At the moment, we lack a complete understanding of the extent to which the introduction of new parts makes systems more or less robust. Thus, we may be building systems likely to produce catastrophic events that we won't see until they hit us. We'll be like islanders playing on the beach while the tsunami, in the form of rapid climate change or financial market collapse, rolls toward shore. New financial instruments—puts, calls, credit default swaps—may have insured the investments of some individuals, but they made financial markets more complex and less transparent. We cannot entrust our future to unsubstantiated beliefs that new financial instruments make the system more robust. To borrow the words of Reinhart and Rogoff (2009), the hope that "this time is different" does not produce robustness.

I want to be clear that the models in this book do not show that diversity guarantees robustness. They do explain some of the mechanisms through which the appropriate kinds of diversity can enhance robustness. Learning what types of diversity to encourage or introduce into a particular system will require data, information, knowledge and wisdom of how that system operates.

We understand a great deal in an absolute sense but very little relative to what can be known about how levels of variation, amounts of diversity, and the heterogeneity of group compositions contribute to complexity. We would be naïve to believe that we can anticipate the systems level effects of artificially changing any one of these, by pulling levers. But we would be equally naïve to take a laissez faire approach to complex systems. It's often said that we shouldn't leave things to chance. Perhaps, it's more appropriate to say that we shouldn't leave things such as our climate, our societies, and our economies to complexity. Better that we try our best to harness complexity (Axelrod and Cohen 2001) and to do that we need to learn more about how complex systems produce the patterns they do (Crutchfield 2009). With that understanding, we might achieve the progress the Alfred North Whitehead describes.

The judicious use of diversity requires moving beyond analogy and metaphor and toward a scientific understanding of the roles that diversity plays. This book has been an initial attempt to lay some foundation for that enterprise. To make breakthroughs, we will need a portfolio of disciplinary approaches (Kitcher 1990; Page 2007a) as well as mutations and recombinations of current ways of thinking: new ideas often require new methodologies.

To be in favor of diversity may be fashionable; and we have many reasons to encourage diversity and to preserve it. Diversity can drive innovation by creating superadditive effects, it can promote system level robustness and flourishing, and sustain all of those gorgeous particulars that make life worth living. But, as should be clear from this book, a scientific and logical approach shows that diversity is no panacea. Too much diversity prevents meaningful structure from emerging; introductions of new species and new products and ideas can destroy as well as create.

The right amount and types of diversity depend on many attributes of a system—connectedness, interdependencies, and rates of adaptation—and they may change over time. Diversity must strike a balance: a balance between exploring and exploiting, a balance between redundancy and novelty, a balance between searching for the new and innovative and simply enjoying the present.

BIBLIOGRAPHY

Alexander, Christopher (2001). *The Phenomenon of Life: Nature of Order, Book 1: An Essay on the Art of Building and the Nature of the Universe (The Nature of Order)*. CES Publishing.

Allesina, S. and Pascual, M. (2009). Googling food webs: Can an eigenvector measure species' importance for coextinctions? *PLoS Computational Biology*, 5(9): 1–6.

Anderson, P. W. (1972). More is different. *Science*, 177(4047).

Arrow, K. J. (1962). The economic implications of learning by doing. *Review of Economic Studies*, 29(3): 155–173.

Arrow, K. J. (1963). *Social Choice and Individual Values*. John Wiley and Son, New York.

Arthur, W. B. (1994). *Increasing Returns and Path Dependence in the Economy*. University of Michigan Press.

Arthur, W. B. (2009). *The Nature of Technology: What It is and How It Evolves*. Free Press.

Ashby, W. R. (1956). *Introduction to Cybernetics*. Chapman & Hall.

Auyang, S. (1998). *Foundations of Complex-Systems Theories in Economics, Evolutionary Biology and Statistical Physics*. Cambridge University Press.

Axelrod, R. (1984). *The Evolution of Cooperation*. Basic Books.

Axelrod, R. (1997). *The Complexity of Cooperation: Agent-Based Models of Competition and Collaboration*. Princeton University Press.

Axelrod, R. and Cohen, M. (2001). *Harnessing Complexity: Organizational Implications of a Scientific Frontier*. Basic Books.

Baldwin, C. Y. and Clark, K. B. (2000). *Design Rules, Vol. 1: The Power of Modularity*. MIT Press.

Barabási, A.-L. (2002). *Linked: The New Science of Networks*. Basic Books.

Barabási, A.-L. (2003). *Linked; How Everything is Connected to Everything Else and What It Means*. Plume.

Barton, R. A. and Harvey, P. H. (2000). Mosaic evolution of brain structure in mammals. *Nature*, 405.

Bednar, J. (2006). Is full compliance possible? Conditions for shirking with imperfect monitoring and continuous action spaces. *Journal of Theoretical Politics*, 18(3): 345–373.

Bednar, J. (2009). *The Robust Federation: Principles of Design*. Cambridge University Press.

Bednar, J., Bramson, A., Jones-Rooy, A., and Page, S. E. forthcoming. Emergent Cultural Signatures and Persistent Diversity: A Model of Conformity and Consistency. *Rationality and Society*.

Bednar, J. and Page, S. E. (2007). Can game(s) theory explain culture? the emergence of cultural behavior within multiple games. *Rationality and Society*, 19(1).

Beinhocker, E. (2006). *The Origin of Wealth: Evolution, Complexity, and the Radical Remaking of Economics*. Harvard University Press.

Bendor, J. (1985). *Parallel Systems: Redundancy in Government*. University of California Press.

Bennett, C. H. (1988). Logical depth and physical complexity. In *The Universal Turing Machine: A Half-century Survey*, edited by R. Herken. Oxford University Press.

Blois, J. L., Feranec, R. S., and Hadly, E. A. (2008). Environmental influences on spatial and temporal patterns of body-size variation in California ground squirrels. *Journal of Biogeography*, 35: 602–613.

Bossert, W., Pattanaik, P. K., and Xu, Y. (2003). Similarity of options and the measurement of diversity. *Journal of Theoretical Politics*.

Brown, J. and West, G. (2000). *Scaling Laws in Biology*. Oxford University Press.

Caswell, H. (1976). Community structure: A neutral model analysis. *Ecological Monographs*, 46: 327–354.

Chaitin, G. (1966a). On the length of programs for computing finite binary sequences. *Journal of the Association for Computing Machinery*, 13.

Chaitin, G. (1966b). On the length of programs for computing finite binary sequences: Statistical considerations. *Journal of the Association for Computing Machinery*, 16.

Chartand, S. (2000). Inventors dream of a world in which no pair of socks is ever mismatched again. New York Times, June 5, 2000.

Clauset, A., Moore, C., and Newman, M. E. J. (2008). Hierarchical structure and the prediction of missing links in networks. *Nature*, 453: 98–101.

Connell, J. H. (1978). Diversity in tropical rain forests and coral reefs. *Science*, 199.

Crutchfield, J. P. (2009). The hidden fragility of complex systems? Consequences of change, changing consequences. In *Cultures of Change: Changing Cultures*, edited by P. Alsina and J. Perello. ACTAR Publishers.

Crutchfield, J. P. and Shalizi, C. (1999). Thermodynamic depth of causal states: objective complexity via minimal representations. *Physical Review E*, 59.

Crutchfield, J. P. and Young, K. (1989). Inferring statistical complexity. *Physical Review Letters*, 63.

Dawkins, R. (1976). *The Selfish Gene.* Oxford University Press.

de Queiroz, K. (2005). Ernst Mayr and the modern concept of species. *Proceedings of the National Academy of Sciences,* 102(1).

Diamond, J. (1999). *Guns, Germs, and Steel: The Fates of Human Societies.* Norton.

Di Falco, S. and Perrings, C. (2003). Crop genetic diversity, productivity and stability of agroecosystems, a theoretical and empirical investigation. *Scottish Journal of Political Economy,* 50(2).

Doak, D. F., Bigger, D., Harding, E. K., Marvier, M. A., O'Malley, R. E., and Thomson, D. (1998). The statistical inevitability of stability-diversity relationships in community ecology. *American Naturalist,* 151(3).

Duranton, G. and Puga, D. (2001). Nursery cities: urban diversity, process innovation, and the life cycle of products. *American Economic Review,* 91(5).

Economo, E. P. and Keitt, T. (2008). Species diversity in neutral metacommunities: a network approach. *Ecology Letters,* 11(1): 52–62.

Edelman, G. M. and Gally, J. A. (2001). Degeneracy and complexity in biological systems. *Proceedings of the National Academy of Sciences,* 98: 13763–13768.

Edwards, A. W. F. (1977). *Foundations of Mathematical Genetics.* 2nd ed. Cambridge University Press.

Ellison, G. (1993). Learning, local Interaction and coordination. *Econometrica,* 61(5): 1047–1071.

Elton, C. S. (1958). *Ecology of Invasions by Animals and Plants.* Chapman & Hall.

Epstein, J. (2006). *Generative Social Science: Studies in Agent-Based Computational Modeling.* Princeton University Press.

Epstein, J. and Axtell, R. (1996). *Growing Artificial Societies: Social Science from the Bottom Up.* MIT Press.

Erwin, D. H. (2001). Lessons from the past: biotic recoveries from mass extinctions. *Proceedings of the National Academy of Sciences*, 98.

Erwin, D. H. (2006). *Extinction: How Life on Earth Nearly Ended 250 Million Years Ago*. Princeton University Press.

Fisher, R. A. (1930). *The Genetical Theory of Natural Selection*. Clarendon Press.

Fodor, J. (1983). *The Modularity of Mind*. MIT Press.

Frank, S. A. (1997). The price equation, fisher's fundamental theorem, kin selection, and causal analysis. *Evolution*, 51(6).

Frank, S. A. and Slatkin, M. (1992). Fisher's fundamental theorem of natural selection. *Trends in Ecology and Evolution*, 7.

Gell-Mann, M. and Lloyd, S. (1996). Information measures, effective complexity, and total information. *Complexity*, 2(1).

Gintis, H. (2007). The dynamics of general equilibrium. *Economic Journal*, 117: 1280–1309.

Gordon, D. M. (1999). *Ants at Work: How an Insect Society is Organized*. Free Press, Simon and Schuster.

Gordon, D. M. (2010). *Ant Encounters: Interaction networks and colony behavior*. Princeton University Press.

Gould, S. J. (1992). *Bully for Brontosaurus: Reflections in Natural History*. Norton.

Gould, S. J. and Lewontin, R. C. (1979). The spandrels of San Marco and the Panglossian paradigm: a critique of the adaptationist programme. *Proceedings of the Royal Society of London B*, 205.

Granovetter, M. (1978). Threshold models of collective behavior. *American Journal of Sociology*, 83(6).

Gravel, N. (2007). What is diversity? In *Rational Choice and Normative Philosophy*, edited by R. Gekker and M. Hees. Routledge.

Grime, J. P. (1973). Competitive exclusion in herbaceous vegetation. *Nature*, 242.

Grzymala-Busse, A. M. (2007). *Rebuilding Leviathan: Party Competition and State Exploitation in Post-Communist Democracies.* Cambridge University Press.

Hamblyn, R. (2001). *The Invention of Clouds: How an Amateur Meteorologist Forged the Language of the Skies.* Farrar Straus & Giroux.

Hardin, G. (1968). The tragedy of the commons. *Science,* 162(3859): 1243–1248.

Harris, D. (2004). Racial classification: the forgotten link between theories and racial conclusion. Paper presented at the annual meeting of the American Sociological Association.

Harrison, D. and Klein, K. (2007). What's the difference? diversity constructs as separation, variety, or disparity in organizations. *Academy of Management Review,* 32(4).

Hobbes, T. (1660). *The Leviathan.*

Holland, J. (1975). *Adaptation in Natural and Artificial Systems.* University of Michigan Press.

Holland, J. (1998). *Emergence: From Chaos to Order.* Helix Books.

Holling, C. S. (1973). Resilience and stability of ecological systems. *Annual Review of Ecology and Systematics,* 4.

Hong, L. and Page, S. E. (2001). Problem solving by heterogeneous agents. *Journal of Economic Theory,* 97: 123–163.

Hong, L. and Page, S. E. (2004). Groups of diverse problem solvers can outperform groups of high-ability problem solvers. *Proceedings of the National Academy of Sciences,* 101(46): 16385–16389.

Huberman, B. A. and Hogg, T. (1986). Complexity and adaptation. *Physica D,* 22.

Hubbell, S. P. (2001). *The Unified Neutral Theory of Biodiversity and Biogeography.* Princeton University Press.

Iwasa, Y., Andreasen, V., and Levin, S. (1987). Aggregation in model ecosystems. I. Perfect aggregation. *Ecological Modeling,* 37: 287–302.

Jacob, F. (1977). Evolution and tinkering. *Science*, 196(4295).

Jain, S. and Krishna, S. (2002). Large extinctions in an evolutionary model: the role of innovation and keystone species. *Proceedings of the National Academy of Sciences*, 99(4): 2055–2060.

Jen, E. (2005). Robust design: a repertoire of biological, ecological, and engineering case studies. In *Santa Fe Institute Studies on the Sciences of Complexity*. Oxford University Press.

Johnson, N. (2003). Personal communication.

Johst, K. and Huth, A. (2005). Testing the intermediate disturbance hypothesis: when will there be two peaks of diversity? *Diversity and Distributions*, 11(1).

Jones, J., Myerscough, M. R., Graham, S., and Oldroyd, B. P. (2004). Honey bee nest thermoregulation: diversity promotes stability. *Science*, 305(5682).

Kauffman, S. (1993). *The Origins of Order: Self-Organization and Selection in Evolution*. Oxford University Press.

Kay, J. (2008). Chapter 1: An introduction to systems thinking. In *The Ecosystem Approach: Complexity, Uncertainty, and Managing for Sustainability*, edited by D. Waltner-Toews, J. Kay, and N.-M. E. Lister. Columbia University Press.

Kimura, M. (1983). *The Neutral Theory of Molecular Evolution*. Cambridge University Press.

Kinouchi, O., Diez-Garcia, R. W., Holanda, A. J., Zambianchi, P., and Roque, A. C. (2008). The nonequilibrium nature of culinary evolution. *New Journal of Physics*, 10: 073020.

Kirman, A. and Vriend, N. (2001). Evolving market structure: an ace model of price dispersion and loyalty. *Journal of Economic Dynamics and Control*, 125.

Kitcher, P. (1990). The division of cognitive labor. *Journal of Philosophy*, 87(1): 5–22.

Koenker, R. and Hallock, K. (2001). Quantile regression: an introduction. *Journal of Economic Perspectives*, 15(4): 143–156.

Kollman, K. (2003). The rotating presidency of the European Council as a search for good policies. *European Union Politics*, 4(1): 51–74.

Kolmogorov, A. (1965). Three appraches to the quantitative definition of information. *Problems in Information Transmission*, 1(1).

Krakauer, D. and Plotkin, J. B. (2002). Principles and parameters of molecular robustness. In *Robust Design*, ed. Erica Jen, Santa Fe Institute Press.

Krakauer, D. C. (2005). Robustness in biological systems: a provisional taxonomy. In *Complex Systems Science in Biomedicine*. Springer.

Langton, C. (1990). Computation at the edge of chaos: phase transitions and emergent computation. *Physica D*, 542.

Lanier, J. (2010). *You are Not a Gadget: A Manifesto*. Knopf.

Lassau, S. A., Hochuli, D. F., Cassis, G., and Reid, C. (2005). Effects of habitat complexity on forest beetle diversity: do functional groups respond consistently? *Diversity Distributions*, 11(1).

Lemonick, M. (2000). Will someone build a perpetual motion machine? *Time Magazine*, April 10.

Leps, J., Osbornova-Kosinova, J., and Rejmanek-Vegetatio, M. (1982). Community stability, complexity and species life history strategies. *Plant Ecology*, 50(1).

Levin, S. (2000). *Fragile Dominion: Complexity and the Commons*. Basic Books.

Lhomme, J. P. and Winkel, T. (2002). Diversity-stability relationships in community ecology: re-examination of the portfolio effect. *Theoretical Population Biology*, 62(3).

Lloyd, S. (2001). Measures of complexity: a non-exhaustive list. *IEEE Control Systems Magazine*, 21.

Lloyd, S. and Pagels, H. (1988). Complexity as thermodynamic depth. *Annals of Physics*, 188.

Lohmann, S. (1994). The dynamics of informational cascades: the Monday demonstrations in Leipzig, East Germany, 1989–91. *World Politics*, 47.

Low, B. S. (2001). *Why Sex Matters: A Darwinian Look at Human Behavior.* Princeton University Press.

MacArthur, R. H. (1955). Fluctuations of animal populations and a measure of community stability. *Ecology*, 36.

MacArthur, R. H. (1960). On the relative abundance of species. *American Naturalist*, 94: 25–36.

MacArthur, R. H. and Wilson, E. O. (1967). *The Theory of Island Bioecography.* Princeton University Press.

Malcolm, J. (2008). *Burdock.* Yale University Press.

March, J. G. (1991). Exploration and exploitation in organizational learning. *Organization Science*, 2.

Matsunaga, T. and Rahman, A. (1998). What brought the adaptive immune system to vertebrates?—the jaw hypothesis and the seahorse. *Immunological Reviews*, 166(1).

May, R. M. (1973). *Stability and Complexity in Model Ecosystems.* Princeton University Press.

May, R. M., Levin, S. A., and Sugihara, G. (2008). Complex systems: ecology for bankers. *Nature*, 451: 893–895.

Mayr, E. (2001). *What Evolution Is.* Basic Books.

McCann, K. (2000). The diversity-stability debate. *Nature*, 405.

McShea, D. and Brandon, R. (2010). *Biology's First Law: The Tendency for Diversity and Complexity to Increase in Evolutionary Systems.* University of Chicago Press.

Meltzer, D. J. (2009). *First Peoples in a New World: Colonizing Ice Age America.* University of California Press.

Miller, J. and Page, S. E. (2008). *Complex Adaptive Systems: An Introduction to Computational Models of Social Life.* Princeton University Press.

Miller, N. (1983). Pluralism and social choice. *American Political Science Review*, 77.

Mitchell, M. (2009). *Complexity: A Guided Tour.* Oxford University Press.

Moorman, A. F. and Christoffels, V. (2003). Cardiac chamber formation: development, genes, and evolution. *Physiological Review*, 83.

Nehring, K. and Puppe, C. (2002). A theory of diversity. *Econometrica*, 70.

Newman, M. E. J. (1997). A model of mass extinction. *Journal of Theoretical Biology*, 189.

Noss, R. (1996). Conservation of biodiversity at the landscape scale. In *Biodiversity in Managed Landscapes: Theory and Practice*, edited by R. Szaro and D. Johnston. Oxford, New York.

Nowak, M. A. and May, R. M. (1992). Evolutionary games and spatial chaos. *Nature*, 359.

Nowak, M. A. and May, R. M. (1993). The spatial dilemmas of evolution. *International Journal of Bifurcation and Chaos*, 3(1).

Odum, E. P. (1953). *Fundamentals of Ecology.* Saunders.

Organski, A. F. K. (1958). *World Politics.* Knopf.

Orrell, D. E. (2007). *The Future of Everything: The Science of Prediction.* Basic Books.

Osame, K., Diez-Garcia, R. W., Holanda, A. J., Zambianchi, P., and Roque, A. C. (2008). The nonequilibrium nature of culinary evolution. arXiv:0802.4393v1.

Osgood, N. (2008). Representing heterogeneity in complex feedback system modeling: computational resource and error scaling. *Proceedings, 22nd International Conference of the System Dynamics Society.* Oxford.

Page, S. E. (2006). Essay: path dependence. *Quarterly Journal of Political Science*, 1: 87–115.

Page, S. E. (2007a). *The Difference: How the Power of Diversity Creates Better Groups, Firms, Schools, and Societies.* Princeton University Press.

Page, S. E. (2007b). Type interaction models and the rule of six. *Economic Theory*, 30(2): 223–241.

Page, S. E. (2008). Uncertainty, difficulty, and complexity. *Journal of Theoretical Politics*, 20.

Page, S. E. and Tassier, T. (2007). Why chains beget chains: an ecological model of firm entry and exit and the evolution of market similarity. *Journal of Economic Dynamics and Control*, 31.

Petroski, H. (1992). *The Evolution of Useful Things*. Vintage Books.

Prahalad, C. K. and Bettis, R. A. (1986). The dominant logic: a new linkage between diversity and performance. *Strategic Management Journal*, 7.

Putnam, R. (2007). E Pluribus Unum: diversity and community in the twenty-first century. *Scandinavian Political Studies*, 30(2): 137–174.

Reinhart, C. M. and Rogoff, K. (2009). *This Time is Different: Eight Centuries of Financial Folly*. Princeton University Press, Princeton, NJ.

Rivkin, J. W. (2000). Imitation of complex strategies. *Management Science*, 46(6).

Ross, E. A. (1920). *The Principles of Sociology*. Century Company.

Roughgarden, J. (1991). The evolution of sex. *American Naturalist*, 183(4).

Rowley, J. (2007). The wisdom hierarchy: representations of the DIKW hierarchy. *Journal of Information Science*, 33(2).

Santos, F. C., Santos, M. D., and Pacheco, J. M. (2008). Social diversity promotes the emergence of cooperation in public goods games. *Nature*, 454.

Schneider, E. D. and Kay, J. (1994). Complexity and thermodynamics. *Futures*, 26(6): 626–647.

Schumpter, J. A. (1942). *Capitalism, Socialism and Democracy*. Harper.

Schweitzer, F., Laxmidhar, B., and Muhlenbein, H. (2002). Evolution of cooperation in a spatial prisoner's dilemma. *Advances in Complex Systems*, 5(2–3).

Seeley, T. (1996). *The Wisdom of the Hive: The Social Physiology of Honey Bee Colonies*. Harvard University Press.

Sharpe, W. F. (1964). Capital asset prices: a theory of market equilibrium under conditions of risk. *Journal of Finance*, 19(3): 425–442.

Shorrocks, B. J., Rosewell, J., Edwards, K., and Atkinson, W. D. (1984). Interspecific competition is not a major organizing force in many insect communities. *Nature*, 310.

Solomonoff, R. (1964). A formal theory of inductive inference part 1 and part 2. *Information and Control 7*, 1–22.

Stearns, S. (1998). *Evolution in Health and Disease*. Oxford University Press.

Stirling, A. (2007). A general framework for analyzing diversity in science, technology, and society. *Journal of the Royal Society: Interface*, 4.

Tews, J., Brose, U., Grimm, V., Tielborger, K., Wichmann, M. C., Schwager, M., and Jeltsch, F. (2004). Animal species diversity driven by habitat heterogeneity/diversity: the importance of keystone structures. *Journal of Biogeography*, 31.

Thompson, D. W. (1992). *On Growth and Form: The Complete Revised Edition*. Dover.

Tilman, D., Knops, J., Wedin, D., Reich, P., Ritchie, M., and Siemann, E. (1997). The influence of functional diversity and composition on ecosystem processes. *Science*, 277(5330): 1300–1302.

Tomiuk, J., Niklasson, M., and Panker, E. D., Jr. (2004). Maintenance of clonal diversity in Dipsa Bifurcata (Fallén, 1810) (diptera:lonchopteridae): II. Diapause stabilizes clonal coexistence. *Heredity*, 93.

Torrens, R. (1815). *An Essay on the External Corn Trade*.

van Someren, M. W., Reimann, P., Boyhuizen, H. P. A., and de Jong, E. B. T. (1998). *Learning with Multiple Representations*. Permagon.

Vincek, V., O'Huigin, C., Satta, Y., Takahata, Y., Boag, P. T., Grant, P. R., Grant, B. R., and Klein, J. (1997). How large was the founding population of Darwin's finches? *Proceedings of the Royal Society: Biological Sciences*, 264(1378).

Wagner, A. (2005). *Robustness and Evolvability in Living Systems*. Princeton University Press.

Watts, D. (1999). *Small Worlds: The Dynamics of Networks between Order and Randomness*. Princeton University Press.

Weber, R. (2006). Managing growth to achieve efficient coordination in large groups. *American Economic Review*, 96(1).

Weitzman, M. (1979). Optimal search for the best alternative. *Econometrica*, 47(3).

Weitzman, M. L. (1992). On diversity. *Quarterly Journal of Economics*, 107(2): 363–405.

Weitzman, M. L. (1998). Recombinant growth. *Quarterly Journal of Economics*, 113(2).

West, G., Brown, J. H., and Enquist, B. J. (1997). A general model for the origin of allometric scaling laws in biology. *Science*, 276(5309).

Whiting, M. F., Bradler, S., and Maxwell, T. (2003). Loss and recovery of wings in stick insects. *Nature*, 421: 264–267.

Whittaker, R. H. (1972). Evolution and measurement of species diversity. *Taxon*, 21: 213–251.

Wolfram, S. (2002). *A New Kind of Science*. Wolfram Media.

Woodwell, G. M. and Smith, H. H. (1969). Diversity and stability in ecological systems. In *22 Brookhaven Symposium on Biology*. Brookhaven National Laboratory.

Wright, S. (1982). The shifting balance theory and macroevolution. *Annual Review of Genetics*, 16.

Yodzis, P. (1981). The stability of real ecosystems. *Nature*, 289.

NOTES

Prelude: The Meaning of Diversity

1. I thank Rajiv Sethi for suggesting this example here.
2. A skeptic might take exception to the claim that complexity is a new phenomenon. Ecosystems have always been complex. Point taken (but only so far). Prior to humans traversing the globe in planes and ships, many species could not escape their local habitats. A thousand years ago, the emerald ash borer had little chance of traveling from China to the United States. Now it can hop aboard a packing crate and wreak havoc, feeding on and destroying every ash tree in my home state of Michigan.

Chapter 1. On Diversity and Complexity

3. Though three classes may seem like plenty, for some applications this categorization proves too crude. Biologists rely on a hierarchical classification into kingdoms, phyla, classes, orders, families, genera, and species.
4. See Levin (2000) for an excellent analysis of "Tragedy of the Commons"–like phenomena in ecosystems.
5. This result was proved independently by Kolmogorov (1965), Chaitin (1966a, b), and Solomonoff (1964).

6. Although, as my colleague Mark Newman has pointed out, we may not be able to distinguish a random sequence from a complex sequence. This is especially true if the complex sequence has been encrypted.

7. Two raised to the ninth power, 2^9, equals 512.

8. In a model of interacting agents with fixed types, I show a trade off between the number of types and the size of groups necessary for any rule based on types to produce multiple equilibria (Page 2007b). This simple model suggests that systems of similar complexity may trade off connectedness with diversity.

9. The analysis that follows borrows heavily from an excellent article by McCann (2000).

10. See also Lep et al. (1982) and McCann (2000).

Chapter 2. Measuring Diversity

11. A less ambitious claim would be that science only demands *orderings*. In this context, an ordering would allow for a ranking of sets by their level of diversity. See Gravel (2007) for a discussion of ordinal approaches to capturing diversity.

12. For example, Bossert et al. (2003) derive axioms that produce Weitzman's (1992) measure, which I cover later in the chapter.

13. Essentialists categorize species by characteristics, geneticists base species on DNA, and populationists draw species boundaries around coherent distinct populations large enough to analyze. This diversity of definitions may be healthy. By emphasizing boundaries, we remain aware of distinct motivating impulses and perspectives. Too much pluralism, though, can undermine good science.

14. The following calculations give this results: $10,000^{0.75} = 1000$, $1^{0.75} = 1$, and $0.05^{0.75} = 0.106$.

15. There exist other measures for specific purposes. Income inequality is often measured by the *Gini coefficient*, which captures the distance of an observed distribution from an equal distribution.

16. Given $2m$ attribute values in the interval $[0, 2]$, variance will be maximized if m of the attributes take value zero and m of the values take value two. In that case, the variance will equal one, and as the mean also equals one, so will the coefficient of variation. That distribution does not maximize the coefficient of variation. It is maximized when $2m - 1$ of the attributes take value zero, and one of the attributes takes value two. In this second distribution, the mean equals $\frac{1}{m}$, the variance equals $\frac{(4m-2)}{m^2}$, and the coefficient of variation equals $(4 - \frac{2}{m})$.

17. See Shorrocks et al. (1984) and Gravel (2007) for more on entropy measures.

18. If the categories have different numbers of types, B can be taken to be the maximum of the number of types without changing the equation.

19. Simpson's index is based on numbers of each type. Let N_i be the number of type i, so that $p_i = \frac{N_i}{N}$. Simpson's index uses $\frac{N_i(N_i-1)}{N N-1}$, which for large N will be approximately p_i^2.

20. The probability of two type ones meeting equals p_1-squared, and so on.

21. Many real world networks do in fact have hierarchical structures and tests; see Clauset et al. (2008).

22. See Nehring and Puppe (2002) for an analysis of conditions under which weighted attribute functions can be constructed given rankings over sets of types.

Chapter 3. The Creation and Evolution of Diversity

23. Wham-O's Richard Knerr and Arthur Melin substituted colorful plastic for bamboo and the rest is history.

24. I take up this problem of too much diversity later in describing the tradeoff between exploration and exploitation.

25. An intuition that should pop to mind about now is that perhaps the number of chromosomes or the genome length (the length of the instructions) corresponds to phenotypic complexity. In other words, are entities with longer instructions more interesting? Using chromosomes is problematic because chromosomes differ in length. Humans have 23 pairs of chromosomes, for a total of forty-six chromosomes. Kangaroos have a mere 12, pigeons have 80 pairs, and algae have 148. Algae may live deep in the ocean but they are not as DEEP as humans. Genome length and species complexity correlate more strongly. Humans have 3.5 billion base pairs, mice have around 2.7 billion, and flies have around 150 million.

26. Drone bees have a single strand of DNA, so they are called *haploid*.

27. I return to this idea in greater detail when discussing the unified neutral theory.

28. See Levin (2000) for a full discussion.

29. Neutral mutation should not be confused with the neutral theory of evolution, which I cover later.

30. If we think of the entities as products, the 0s and 1s could denote the presence or absence, respectively, of attributes. Fitness would be profitability.

31. Though Darwin's finches are often described as an example of a *founder effect*, evidence suggests the initial populations had to be fairly large (Vincek et al. 1997).

32. In fact, squirrel size does vary with environmental factors. Blois et al. (2008) show that the size variation of squirrels can be explained by the rainfall patterns. This explains why northern California squirrels are larger than those in southern California.

33. I'm drawing a bright line here between contextual and proficient adaptations. Biologists may find this statement puzzling (if not wrong). Almost all adaptations that biologists study are contextual to some degree. However, that's not true in the social and economic realms. Organizations learn how to produce their products more efficiently over time, reducing cost and waste. Those adaptations are entirely proficient. Furthermore, even in the biological realm, some adaptations, such as adaptations that allow birds to fly farther using less energy without loss of speed, may be nearly proficient.

34. See Frank and Slatkin (1992) for a discussion of this point.

35. If people make errors when coordinating or if they desire consistency across domains, then cultures will exhibit variation (see Bednar et al. forthcoming).

36. Over a large area, spatially constrained disturbances would produce both grassy patches and heavily forested patches.

37. Note that with these rules, with probability $\frac{4}{10}$ times $\frac{3}{11}$ the boundary will become ragged: BBBBBABAAAAA.

38. I'm describing a simple Markov process.

39. Interested readers can see Page and Tassier (2007) for a deeper analysis.

40. In some contexts, particularly in complex systems, it may be difficult for individuals to determine the cause of success so reproduction of the fittest isn't as easy as it might seem (Rivkin 2000).

Chapter 4. Constraints on Diversity

41. If the X_i differ, the formula can be written as $\prod_{i=1}^{D} X_i$.

42. The dimensionality/cardinality framework has limitations. To calculate the diversity of possible partitionings of reality—the placing of objects into categories—we must count the number

of subsets of a set. This number, called the Bell number, grows very fast. It's not of the form X^D. I take this up in a later chapter.

43. I'll return to power laws when I cover the Central Limit Theorem. There, I'll be discussing power law distributions in which the exponent z is less than negative one. Those distributions have lots of large events.

44. See Caswell (1976) for a precursor to this model.

45. Why this is true isn't *that* complicated. Jumping ability depends on angle of flexure, density of mass, number of legs, and proportions that depend on body shape; see www.applet-magic.com/darcy.htm for a full explanation.

46. Though crude, simple plus/minus approaches often prove quite accurate predictors.

Chapter 5. Variation in Complex Systems

47. This derivation follows the excellent characterization of the Price theorem by Frank (1997).

48. In the statement of the Price equation, $Cov[x, y]$ equals the covariance of the random variables x and y.

49. This model simplifies Weitzman (1979), in which he considers the general model of how to choose from distributions.

50. This can be done formally as follows: let $\Theta_{t+1} = \Theta_t + \epsilon_t$, where ϵ_t is a random variable.

51. See Miller and Page 2008 for an expanded version of the how negative and positive feedbacks determine stability.

52. Of course, one can also argue the flip side of this argument—that a precondition for war would be that the balance of power must be nearly equal. Only when power is nearly equal would either party initiate a war. Otherwise, why would the weaker country not just acquiesce? In this theory, called *power*

transition theory, the instigator of a war would most often be a weaker state that's on the rise, a state that's approaching power parity (Organski 1958).

Chapter 6. Diversity's Inescapable Benefits I: Averaging

53. In a more general model, factor i could influence a different number of entities.

Chapter 7. Diversity's Inescapable Benefits II: Diminishing Returns to Types

54. Dates and bananas both grow on palms, though in common usage we sometimes say banana tree and date palm. Here, I refer to both as trees.
55. Interactions are not the same thing as *nonlinearities*. Functions with decreasing returns are nonlinear but need not include interaction effects.

Chapter 8. Diversity's Impact in Complex Systems

56. In the table, Aisha's output of fish is computed as follows: multiply 160 lbs per month times the portion of the month, $\frac{3}{5}$ to get 96 lbs.
57. To show the result formally, let $N = 2n - 1$. Then it can be shown that the ratio of per capita productivity under specialization to per capita productivity under generalization exceeds

$$R(N) = \frac{\left(\Pi_{t=1}^{k}(1 + \frac{r}{tn})\right)^{N}}{\left(\Pi_{t=1}^{k}(1 + \frac{r}{tN})\right)^{N}}.$$

It follows that $\lim_{N \to \infty} R(N) = \infty$.

58. There are of course risks to specialization. If the system breaks up, agents may get stuck with a single skill and prove unable to produce all the goods necessary to survive. But here I am focusing on efficiency.

59. In the case of human immune systems, these differences in immunity can be extreme. Meltzer (2009) describes how the epidemiologist Francis Black has estimated the probability of a virus not encountering a new antigen of a particular type as it moves from one Native American to another to be approximately one-third. The probability that the same virus would not meet a different antigen of that type when passing between European Americans would be less than 1 percent.

60. Recall that the common component eradicates eight viruses of length five.

61. Think of each possible method as either included or not. This creates a binary string of length k, with 1 denoting included and 0 denoting not included. There are 2^k binary strings of length k, but we have to subtract the string of all zeros, leaving $2^k - 1$ possibilities. Of course, not all combinations of tricks will work on all problems. Suppose that our problem is to make a sandwich. My tricks may include "add peanut butter" and "add pickles." In some cases, each of these tricks may work, but seldom do both.

62. When doing a formal statistical analysis of this model, I averaged over all two thousand starting points.

63. Given that the agents try their heuristics sequentially, the heuristics $\{2, 13, 7\}$ and the heuristics $\{2, 7, 13\}$ won't necessarily get stuck at the same point.

64. For the formal conditions see Hong and Page (2004). These include the fact that all of the problem solvers must only get stuck at a countable number of solutions.

65. See Arthur (2009) for detailed examples of this process.

66. This phenomenon is often referred to as collective wisdom.

67. In Page (2007), I refer to prediction variance as diversity to call attention to the fact that it's created by diverse partitions.
68. Source for fire departments: FEMA http://www.usfa.dhs.gov/statistics/departments/index.shtm
69. A network has a uniform distribution of connections if each object has the same probability of being connected to every other object.
70. See Bendor (1985).

Chapter 9. Parting Thoughts

71. A similar logic holds in ecosystems. Species selected for fitness, just like individuals motivated by wealth or prestige, tend to take actions for their own good, not for the collective good.

INDEX